TRUE RELATIONSHIP

TRUE RELATIONSHIP

a detailed roadmap to strategic compatibility

SANTTU ROY

Dear Readers

Welcome to *True Relationship*, a journey into the profound influence of relationships on our lives. Relationships act as powerful mentors, guiding us through growth, transformation, and at times, testing our sanity. They are essential in shaping who we are, teaching us life's most complex lessons, and showing us how to balance our inner harmony by connecting with the right people for the right reasons.

As you begin reading, consider how your own experiences—moments of love, challenges, and connection—shape your perspective. Your personal journey, alongside your curiosity about relationships, has led you here. Whether you are nurturing a current relationship, healing from a past one, or seeking new and meaningful connections, this book invites you to explore those paths deeply.

One of the book's unique aspects lies in the fascinating story of wolves and their relationships—a powerful parallel that shows how the animal kingdom offers insights into loyalty, connection, and communal strength. Wolves, with their close bonds, communication, and ability to navigate life's seasons as a pack, embody the instinctual wisdom we learn from in our own relationships.

My love for numerology and astrology shapes this journey, adding an exploration of how cosmic patterns and the energies of numbers reflect our connections and compatibility. This perspective encourages a deeper look at how we align with others, showing relationships as more than what meets the eye –they are part of a broader, universal rhythm.

Use this book as a guide to enrich your own journey. Each chapter offers strategies, without needing to read from start to finish. Start by choosing chapters that speak to you right now. Reflect on the ideas and insights that resonate, allowing them to influence your perspective and actions in your relationships.

I have dedicated my heart and writing to this book with the hope that it serves as a meaningful resource for you. May it help you strengthen connections, find balance, and understand the intricate beauty of relationships in new ways.

With heartfelt intentions, Santtu Roy.

Table Of Content

Chapter 1 : Introduction 9

Chapter 2: Essential Considerations.....................17

Chapter 2 : Numerology Compatibility................21

Chapter 3 : Karmic Numbers 97

Chapter 4 : Vedic Astrology................................101

Chapter 5 : Astro-numerology 147

Chapter 6 : Basic Character Traits.......................285

Chapter 1 : Introduction

In the wild, wolves embody an unwavering commitment that offers a remarkable lesson for human relationships. Unlike many animals, wolves form bonds that last a lifetime. Wolves, both male and female, have an innate sense that their partnership lasts a lifetime. From a young age, they start getting ready by learning and practicing the actions needed for a lasting and harmonious relationship. Once they make a decision on a partner, it's with a commitment to their family's future, not just for themselves.

As parents, wolves dedicate themselves wholly to raising and protecting their young. They create an environment of care, structure, and guidance, teaching their offspring how to navigate the wild and survive. Each partner plays a role, supporting one another in tasks essential for the pack's survival. This shared dedication reinforces their bond, showing that a strong relationship rests on a foundation of trust, responsibility, and mutual effort.

The portrayal of wolves demonstrating lifelong loyalty, nurturing their family, and achieving success as a unit, establishes a framework for understanding human relationships. Like wolves, we understand that lasting bonds need both preparation and commitment. From the wolves' sense of purpose and teamwork, we can derive inspiration for our own lives. What is the real essence of establishing a significant, strategic partnership among people? How can we build relationships that mirror the resilience and harmony seen in nature?

This leads us to consider the journey to strategic compatibility in our relationships–a path where love evolves from fleeting attraction to a purposeful, enduring union.

The Journey to Strategic Compatibility

True Relationship: A Detailed Roadmap to strategic compatibility offers a fresh perspective on the journey of love, shedding light on the path to a meaningful and enduring union. Love often brings us to crossroads where we must choose between the thrill of new experiences and the depth of a long-term commitment. Marriage and partnerships are not just social contracts; they represent a fusion of practicality and spirituality that shapes our lives.

Relationships require active participation and deliberate effort to foster connection and growth. It's about inviting people into your life who uplift and nourish you and about cultivating the skills for a healthy, fulfilling partnership.

Even without realising, we often possess a natural understanding of these principles through subtle cues and initial perceptions, leading us to people who share our values. The advice to "trust those who understand you" or "beware of those who avoid eye contact" is based on intuition and helps build meaningful relationships.

This book unveils the profound potential within every relationship, offering a pathway to lifelong love and commitment. Through a series of insightful questions and engaging exercises, it guides couples to deepen their connection, fostering trust, understanding, and shared purpose for:

Open Communication

- Lay all your cards on the table

- Be honest

- Spend time with each other's family

- Commit for the long haul

- Understand each other's values

Discovering Personal Preferences

- Take an engagement-moon trip

- Have the money talk

- Discuss plans for children

- Meet each other's favourite people

- Explore interests and tastes

- Does your partner like to read?

- What kind of music do they listen to?

- How do they feel about social media?

- Are they a dog person or a cat person?

- What TV shows do they enjoy?

- What's the best present they've ever given you?

- What kind of food do they prefer?

- What hobbies do they have?

- Do you get along with their closest friends?

- What's their clothing style?

"Marriage is not a noun; it's a verb. It isn't something you get. It's something you do. It's the way you love your partner every day." – Barbara De Angelis

Understanding Beliefs

- Is your partner religious?

- Do they make life decisions based on their religious beliefs?

- Do they expect you to participate in their religion?

- Is it an issue if you have different spiritual beliefs?

Political Alignment

- Does your partner care about political issues?

- Do you belong to the same ideological party?

- Is it an issue if your political ideals differ?

- Do their political beliefs impact their decisions?

"The success of marriage comes not in finding the 'right' person, but in the ability of both partners to adjust to the real person they inevitably realize they married." – John Fischer

Career and Life Aspirations

- Does your partner enjoy their work?

- How important is your relationship to them?

- Who are the most important people in their life?

- Are they engaged with current events?

- Do they volunteer?

- Who do they value spending time with most?

- What does it look like when they deeply care about something?

Family Planning

- Do you both want children?

- Where would you like to raise kids?

- When would you like to start a family?

- How would you handle pregnancy and potential challenges?

- Are you open to alternative paths to parenthood?

- Their childhood and parental relationships?

- What parenting style do they envision?

- How many children do they want?

- What are their childcare preferences?

Career Goals

- Aligning career aspirations

- Ensuring support and shared objectives in your

Lifestyle Preferences

- Discussing overall lifestyle preferences

- Balancing alone time, family time, and hobbies

- Budget and spending habits

Intimate Connection

- Prioritising your sex life

- Communicating effectively about intimate needs

- Keeping your sex life exciting

"A successful marriage requires falling in love many times, always with the same person." – Mignon McLaughlin

Navigating Diverse Beliefs and Practices

- Understanding each other's cultural backgrounds, including traditions and social norms

- Acknowledging and discussing differences in beliefs and finding common ground

- Exploring the impact of each other's religious practices and beliefs

- Discussing career aspirations and the role of work in your lives

- Embracing and celebrating each other's cultural festivals and traditions

- Navigating language differences and communication

- Sharing and appreciating each other's cuisine

- Understanding extended family dynamics

- Adapting to different social etiquettes

- Exploring cultural roots through travel

- Combining traditions creatively

- Developing conflict resolution strategies with cultural sensitivities in mind

- Integrating both cultures in parenting

- Recognising support from cultural communities

- Continual learning about each other's culture

In a true relationship, navigating cultural change through marriage calls for an open heart and a patient spirit. It's a commitment to honor and embrace each partner's unique heritage and the diversity they bring. This journey of mutual growth fosters a richer, more harmonious connection, blending shared beliefs, values, and philosophies. It's about finding alignment not only in practical aspects, like careers and lifestyles, but also in the deeper, evolving values that shape life together. Marriage is not a static state—it's a dynamic partnership that flourishes through understanding, adaptation, and the shared journey of two lives becoming one.

Chapter 2: Essential Considerations

As we start our marriage, we must know it's more than romance. It's a lifelong commitment. It requires a deep alignment of values, beliefs, and goals. "True Relationship" helps you with key points. It fosters a union that aligns body and soul in perfect sync.

Marriage is a deep, lasting institution. It is more than a social contract. It is a spiritual and emotional partnership that goes beyond companionship. A strong, lasting relationship needs some key elements. They would create a fulfilling, lasting union. This chapter covers key aspects to help you and your partner. It seeks to build a bond of trust and respect, with shared goals.

Open Communication

Effective communication is the bedrock of any successful relationship. To build a strong partnership, be open and honest. Share your values, beliefs, and future goals. This openness fosters trust and strengthens your bond. Have meaningful talks. Meet each other's families. Discuss blend of different subject other than your profession. This practice builds a solid foundation. It also ensures both partners remains aligned.

Discovering Personal Preferences

Knowing your partner's preferences is key. It helps you respect and celebrate differences in the relationship. Explore each other's interests and hobbies. Connect by honouring these unique aspects. Plan an "engagement-moon" trip. It helps you bond and discuss finances and future plans. Knowing what makes your partner tick would help. Learn their favourite music and views on social media. This helps you avoid conflicts and create a better daily life.

Understanding Beliefs

Beliefs shape our identities and influence our decisions. It's vital to know how your partner's beliefs affect their choices. These might be religious, spiritual, or personal. Share ideas freely in group conversations. These beliefs may affect your relationship. Respecting these differences and finding common ground would guide you how to collaborate when opinion differs.

Career and Life Aspirations

Aligning career goals and life aspirations is fundamental to a harmonious relationship. Discuss your career goals, work-life balance, and supporting each other. Aligning your career goals with your partner's would build a strong future together.

Family Planning

Speaking about family planning is crucial when building a future together. Talking about your wish to have children is part of this. It covers parenting difficulties and where to raise a family. Sync up on this crucial life choice. Recognise one another's parenting philosophies, customs, and standards for raising children.

Lifestyle Alignment

Lifestyle preferences play a critical role in maintaining harmony within a relationship. Discuss your lifestyle. Include how you spend your time, manage finances, and focus on your relationship. Aligning these preferences prevents conflicts and contribute to a fulfilling partnership.

Intimate Connection

A happy and open private life is a prerequisite for a successful marriage. Examine your close relationship and talk about your personal erotic desires. Meeting one another's needs strengthens your relationship. It supports desires and enthusiasm.

Navigating Diverse Beliefs and Practices

In our interconnected world, cultural and belief differences are common. We must respect and understand each other's cultures, traditions, and beliefs. It means bridging language gaps, sharing cuisines, and adapting traditions for a shared experience. Embracing these differences could enrich your relationship and create a more resilient partnership.

Conflict Resolution

Conflicts remains natural in every relationship. But how we handle them defines our marriage's success. Develop conflict resolution strategies. They must respect cultures, beliefs, and emotions. To build trust, address conflicts with empathy and understanding.

This chapter explores the key points for a lasting, happy relationship. By addressing these areas, we and our partner could build a great marriage. This sets the stage for a lifetime of love, growth, and happiness.

Chapter 2 : Numerology Compatibility

At her kitchen table, Olivia reads *Unlocking Your Destiny*, a book on numerology, eager as her wedding to Ethan, her fiancé, approaches in a week. She explores every angle to deepen their bond, captivated by the ancient belief as numbers carries vibrational frequencies influencing life and relationships. Olivia seeks insights into her compatibility with Ethan through numerology, recognizing how it can reveal partners' strengths, anticipate challenges, and clarify relationship dynamics. This method, based on names and birth dates, offers a numerical perspective supports in strengthening bonds and reveal character traits.

Numerology divides people into nine unique personality and life path numbers, with each number from 1 to 9 carrying distinct meanings. These numbers reflect a person's character and their relationships. For Olivia and Ethan, numerology reveals intriguing aspects of their personalities: Olivia's Life Path number 7 makes her introspective and spiritual, drawn to life's deeper mysteries. Ethan's Life Path number 5 embodies an adventurous, free-spirited energy. Their shared love for exploration and respect strengthens their connection.

The book explores the compatibility of Life Path 7 and 5 individuals, noting that while this pairing has both rewards and challenges, it creates balance. Olivia learns that her introspective nature could help ground Ethan's adventurous spirit, while his spontaneity encourages her to embrace change.

Olivia realizes numerology is not a definitive guide but a valuable tool for assessing relationship dynamics. It offers a fresh perspective on their compatibility, reminding her that love is not solely about harmony but about growing together through differences. While the numbers hint at compatibility, they are part of a larger picture.

With newfound clarity, Olivia closes the book, feeling a surge of excitement for the wedding. Numerology deepens understanding of her relationship with Ethan, emphasising love involves growth, understanding, and celebrating their unique journey together.

This chapter provides fundamental advice on numerology compatibility, offering couples a practical way to assess their relationship. With a few calculations, it offers insights into compatibility before seeking professional numerology guidance. Destiny number, name number, zodiac sign, birth date, and personality number all contribute to a unique understanding of one's bond, helping couples see their relationship more clearly.

For centuries, people have trusted numerology. It reveals insights into compatibility between individuals. Numerology can help you understand and improve your relationship. It's a unique way to view it, whether you're preparing for marriage or not.

9 Years Cycles (7-9)

In numerology, the 9-year cycle represents a repeating sequence of personal growth and transformation. Each year within this cycle has a unique theme and purpose, guiding individuals through phases of development, learning, and renewal. The journey begins in a "Year 1," which focuses on new beginnings, setting intentions, and initiating fresh projects or paths. It progresses through phases of building, nurturing, challenges, personal growth, and reflection, each year building upon the last.

The final stage, "Year 9," symbolises completion, letting go, and preparing for the start of a new cycle. During this time, individuals reflect on the journey, release outdated habits or relationships, and clear the way for the next cycle's opportunities. This sequence repeats every nine years, providing a rhythm for personal and spiritual evolution

1. Beginning (Year 1): Commencing with a sense of independence and individuality, Year 1 marks a fresh start where possibilities are endless.

2. Connecting (Year 2): Year 2 shifts focus to relationships, emphasising cooperation and diplomacy for forging meaningful connections.

3. Creating (Year 3): Marked by creativity and self-expression, Year 3 unfolds as ideas take shape, and artistic endeavours flourish.

4. Building (Year 4): Stability and structure define Year 4, a period dedicated to laying foundations in both personal and professional domains.

5. Changing (Year 5): The midway point brings transformation and adaptability, urging individuals to embrace change with an open mind.

6. Nurturing (Year 6): Year 6 embodies nurturing and responsibility, focusing on family, home, and community with compassion and harmony.

7. Reevaluating (Year 7): A year of introspection and analysis, Year 7 prompts spiritual growth and reassessment of life's path.

8. Expanding (Year 8): Signifying expansion and achievement, Year 8 encourages embracing opportunities for growth and abundance.

9. Completing (Year 9): The final year symbolises endings and closure, inspiring reflection on the journey and making way for new beginnings..

Numbers

Numbers by themselves have no inherent meaning, but they gain significance through various

disciplines like mathematics, accounting, and numerology.

Every number from 1 to 9 has its own meaning, and each letter in the alphabet corresponds to a number between 1 and 9, which also has significance. The number 9 is seen as the peak because

numerology works on a nine-year cycle.

Each subsequent number builds on the last, expressing different aspects like independent (1),

relationships (2), creativity (3), stability (4), freedom (5), responsibility (6), introspection (7),

material success (8), and humanitarianism (9).

Even: 2, 4, 6, 8

Odd: 1, 3, 5, 7, 9

Numerology has many interpretations of each number. One-digit numbers are easier to work with. They have a clearer meaning. It's easier to piece together a personality puzzle with them. add and reduce the birthday number to a single digit, except 11, 22 and reveal the individual's insights.

Zero (0)

It enables exponential growth when combined with other numbers and embodies both nothingness and limitless potential, balancing creation and destruction 

Zero is a starting point for new possibilities. It represents nothingness. But, adding it to other numbers causes exponential growth (e.g. 10, 1000, 10000). Zero has limitless applications.

But, it often focuses on the growth or decay of matter. It shows qualities like intensity, power, and creation. It also takes and gives.

One (1)

1 is the base of the other numbers, a leader who stands straight and confident.

A person represented by the number 1 dislikes authorities because he or she strives to become an authority themselves. Because there is no one else to support them, they stay bound by their innate ego and impulses.

Courage, ambition, and confidence drive the quest for success.

1 stands alone like a self-reliant, dominant lamppost. It is a leader. The Sun's energy, vibration, and strength influence individuals born on the 1st, 10th, 19th, and 28th of any month.

The planet Sun governs the number 1 and represents activity. It has knowledge of what will happen, as well as the guts, boldness, determination, and wisdom to move to a location where everything is blank and empty.

Positive Qualities

- Resourcefulness
- Individuality
- Leadership through innovation
- Self-assurance

- Strong beliefs

Negative Traits

- Selfishness

- Introverts

- Aggression

- Dominance

- Impulsiveness

Two (2)

2 represents pairs, duality, adaptability, wholeness, flexibility, and harmony.

Considering number one (1) as an independent man, consider number two (two) as a woman.

The planet Moon rules the 2.

Those born on the 2nd, 11th, 20th, and 29th enjoy all the qualities of this planet. Those with this energy exhibit a balance of romanticism and domesticity. They show tenderness, kindness, and no aggression or dominance. They can understand and appreciate both sides of an issue. This enables them to tackle problems with balanced judgment and receptivity.

Their intuition helps them manage differences and disagreements. It keeps them calm in tough situations.

Positive Qualities

- Duality
- Facilitator
- Diplomacy
- Integrity
- Spiritual

Negative Traits

- Predominant mind
- Indifferent
- Careless
- Unsociable
- Unable to make up his/her mind

Three (3)

In numerology, the number 3 holds significant importance as it is the first digit in the Heavenly Triad, which comprises the numbers 3, 6, and 9. Jupiter governs those born on the 3rd, 12th, 21st, and 30th of the month. Its integrity brings in imagination, procreation, motion, thought, a certain amount of luck and magic.

Individuals with the number 3 have a strong desire to accomplish their goals, they are child like, master of material achievement through creative ability and expression. People with a birthday number of 3 exhibit creativity, enthusiasm, quick wit, and humour. They can uplift those around them.

Jupiter linked to the number three. So, this energy helps young people with their education, growth, and careers. They can express themselves well. They may excel in art, music, writing, or acting. The number 3 means growth and expansion. It is a good number for business and personal growth.

Positive Qualities

- Curiosity and joyous
- Self-expression
- Empathetic
- Creative communication
- Consciousness, and positivity
- Satisfaction

Negative Traits

- Obsessions
- Selfish
- Sensual
- Unresponsive
- Lack of motivation

Four (4)

4 represents management, regularity, and practicalityIn numerology, consider those who born on 4th, 13th, 22nd and 31st of the month as four.

A person with a birthday number of 4 stays practical, reliable, hard-working, honest and known for their self-discipline.

Understanding them takes time as they appear intense, fearful, worried, and confused.

Also, the number four (4) means repetitive stability, hard work, productivity, and well-being. It includes rules, techniques, dependability, and strength.

The 4 want to revolutionise with new ideas. But most people hate new ideas. They take them outside their comfort zones.

Positive Qualities

- Attention and consistency
- Rationality
- Realism
- Sincerity
- Persistence, and foundation

Negative Traits

- Unplanned, lack of imagination

- Excessive seriousness

- Tremendous detail

- Stubbornness

- Fixed viewpoints, misunderstanding

Five (5)

The planet Mercury influences people born on 5th, 14th, and 23rd of the month. The number Five (5) sits at the centre of 1 to 10, it shows the balanced symbol, administration, and control over the condition.

People represented by the number 5 are natural speakers. They have great social skills and they get along with everyone. Those with number 5 described as adventurous and thrive for environments that are constantly changing.

5 is a balanced number, as it occupies the middle ground between extremes.

The numbers 5 and 3 share charm, relationships, and communication skills. As a result, we regard people with a 5 personality as pleasing. There is a connection between the number 5 and freedom and versatility. The number 5 has an affinity for a curious mind.

Positive Qualities

- Action oriented
- Administration
- Promoting ideas
- Freedom loving
- Quickness, and curiosity

Negative Traits

- Anxiousness
- Unhappiness
- Mood Swing
- Sharp Speech
- Temper, dissatisfaction, impatience

Six (6)

The number 6 is the second number in the trinity 3, 6, and 9. Those born on 6th, 15th, or 24th of the month bear the quality of number 6 under the planet Venus. A birthday number 6 is someone who prefers a strong family bonding.

Individuals born with a 6 birthday number focus on family ties and unity. They are artistic and idealistic. They want to nurture and comfort others.

They often rank the happiness of their loved ones. They strive to create a supportive, harmonious environment for those around them. It is the vibration of a home seeker, returning home, flying back to the nest, seeking shelter from the storm. It is the vibration of warmth and security.

The 6 energy is associated with love for children, animals, and music.

Positive Qualities

- Artistic
- Visionary, humanist
- Truth, and righteousness
- Family values, family loving
- Conventional, and welfare

Negative Traits

- Compassionate
- Commitment
- Obscenity, and outspokenness
- Timidity, and slowness in decision-making
- Stubbornness
- Complaint, egoistic

Seven (7)

The number 7 symbolises insight, the search for deeper meaning in things, and those represents the number 7 have many deep thoughts in their mind. The number 7 governs those born on the 7th, 16th, and 25th of the month, while Neptune is the rolling planet for number 7 in west, but in Vedic system its Ketu.

They characterise a person with a birthday number of 7 as analytical, a decision making and private care giver.

The number 7 own intelligence, logical ideas, and a analysing brain. This number brings in mystical questions and why there are 7 colours of the rainbow, 7 chakra, 7 days in a week and 7 notes on the scale of a piano.

A direct and varied life experience coupled with deep, intellectual aim, and spiritual thought is the only way to reach number 7. We must acknowledge its potential, honour it, respect it and utilise it. The number is protected to prevent it from being seen or understood.

Positive Qualities

- Technology, and science
- Analytical abilities
- Exploration
- Computation
- Occultist, dignity, and perfectionist

- Manner, and personality

Negative Traits

- Sentimental intelligence

- Isolation, and resentment

- Reserve, and skepticism

- Disproportionate, and over-analysis

- Temper, and individualism, critical views

Eight (8)

For those born on the 8th, 17th, or 26th, their number is 8. The planet Saturn governs this number.

Number 8 individuals have a natural talent for managing money. They can oversee large projects with ambition and authority. They value discipline and persevere through life's hardships.

They desire to succeed and can manage challenges, driving them.

Eight (8) focuses on balancing between the material and spiritual world.

When it is a source of power and strength, the number 8 also refers to money. Research and study people with this number in their chart or life path. It leads to wealth or power. Wealthy individuals are more likely to have the number 8.

Positive Qualities

- Responsibility
- Attention to detail
- Efficiency and supervision
- Execution ability, and operational performance
- Awareness, judgement, and organisation

Negative Traits

- Tiredness
- Unable to focus
- Overreaction, and tension
- Repressing others
- Demanding, and commanding

Nine (9)

In the trinity of 3, 6, and 9, the number 9 is the final number. It is a divine number, and represents selflessness, compassion, and humanitarianism. Influenced by this number, they have a profound grasp of human nature. Helping others is something they are strongly driven to do. They are believed to have strong intuition and a deep connection to the universe.

On the other hand, the number 9 is often connected to endings and closures. It symbolises the end of one phase and the importance of making space for new beginnings.

The number nine (9) is under the influence of Mars, and those born on the 9th, 18th, or 27th are influenced by its energy.

They possess a great determination to achieve success, as they appear thoughtful, accepting, and hardworking. They have the potential to be either the administrator or the leader.

Positive Traits

- Love, perfection and taking action
- Ideality, and compassion
- Humanitarianism, and philanthropy
- Forgiveness, and leaders in charitable activity
- Artistic, writers, and musicians

Negative Traits

- Too much aggression
- Self-centredness
- Impulsiveness, and possessiveness
- Demanding, and mood swings
- Inability to use talents
- Carelessness

Eleven (11)

11/2, and 22/4 are master numbers. A master number is a double-digit-number repeats itself and comes from a single root number. The number 11 is a master number with 1 repeated and the reduced number is 2 (1 + 1 = 2) a root number.

The number 11/2 referred as the spiritual messenger, as they show deep commitment to bringing spiritual messages to Earth. An 11/2's we perceive good energy as motivating and uplifting, as well as intuitive, sensitive, and too exuberant.

The numerology master number 11/2 symbolises the interplay between masculine and feminine, active and receptive energies, signifying that two individuals traverse the space to achieve balance. The two pillars of a gateway represent this compound number, with the centre point between them signifying a choice towards a positive, upward path. Success will follow if one is on the correct path.

Positive Qualities

- Inspirational
- Intuitive
- Intellectual
- Innovative and Creative
- Co-operative

Negative Traits

- Egocentric

- Depressive

- Overly sensitive

- Susceptible to stress

Twenty -Two (22)

People have labeled the number twenty-two (22/4) as the master builder. 22/4 people, are a planner, builder and a visionary who could see "big picture" through smaller details. 

They may work as musicians, composers, interpreters, instructors, ministers, painters, and decorators, among other professions. They love to share, encourage, and uplift other people.

Those with   22/4 know how to combine inspirational ideas with physique, and they bring the ability to show.

Yet 22 is less effective than the 11, indeed adaptable to the earth's plane; it manifest material success since its root is 4.

You could see a 22/4 as the force behind great undertakings as they are deft organisers and ambitious workers. Other higher vibrations associated with the 22/4 are idealism, intuition, confidence and wisdom.

Positive Qualities

- Revolutionary
- Ambitious
- Intelligent
- Realistic
- bursting with potential

Negative Traits

- Egocentric
- Depressive
- Overly sensitive
- Susceptible to stress
- Emotionally controlled
- Insensitive

Planets

Numerology gives importance to the Navagrahas, or the nine planets, as they shape our lives and fate. Every planet has its own unique energy, influence, and a profound effect on our personality, relationships, and life.

Besides nine planets, Vedic numerology includes the influence of Rahu and Ketu, the two shadow planets, in shaping our lives and destiny.

The Sun (Surya) represents our individuality, ego, and self-expression. It holds immense power and is associated with leadership, creativity, and vitality.

The Moon (Chandra) symbolises our emotions, intuition, and subconscious mind. It is related to nurturing, sensitivity, and creativity.

Mars (Mangal) represents our passion, energy, and ambition. It is associated with courage, aggression, and determination.

Mercury (Budha) the planet Mercury mirrors our communication skills, intellect, and analytical abilities. It is associated with adaptability, versatility, and mental agility.

Jupiter (Guru) Jupiter is our wisdom, knowledge, and spirituality. It is associated with growth, abundance, and expansion.

Venus (Shukra) the planet Venus shows our love, relationships, and creativity. It is associated with beauty, harmony, and sensuality.

Saturn (Shani) Saturn is our discipline, responsibility, and hard work. It is associated with challenges, obstacles, and lessons.

Rahu (North node) a shadow planet that is our desires and ambitions. It is associated with materialism, obsession, and illusion.

Ketu (South node) another shadow planet that describes our spirituality and detachment. It is associated with detachment, liberation, and enlightenment.

Numbers and week-days

- Sunday: 1 - 4
- Monday: 2 - 7
- Tuesday: 9
- Wednesday: 5
- Thursday: 3
- Friday: 6
- Saturday: 8

Numbers and Planets

- Sun: 1
- Moon: 2
- Jupiter: 3
- Rahu / Uranus: 4
- Mercury: 5
- Venus: 6
- Ketu / Neptune: 7
- Saturn: 8
- Mars: 9

Planet's Characteristics

1	SUN	Light
8	SAT	Dark
2	MO	Attachment
7	KE	Detachment
3	JU	God's Guru
6	VE	Demon's Guru
4	RA	Malefic
5	ME	Benefic

Peaceful	Hostile
JUP	SUN
VEN	SAT
Waxing MON	MAR
MER	Waning MON
	RAH
	KET

Day	Night	All Time
JUP	KET	MER
RAH	MON	
SUN	MAR	
VEN	SAT	

Day of Month

This is a summary of the traits of people born on specific days of the month.

1: Individuals born on the 1st of the month possess pure Sun energy and tend to be independent, self-motivated, assertive, and natural leaders.

2: Individuals born on the 2nd of the month possess pure Moon energy and tend to be sensitive, cooperative, diplomatic, and intuitive.

3: Individuals born on the 3rd of the month possess pure Jupiter energy and tend to be creative, expressive, optimistic, and social.

4: Individuals born on the 4th of the month possess pure Rahu/Uranus energy and tend to be practical, disciplined, hardworking, and reliable..

5: Individuals born on the 5th of the month possess pure Mercury energy and tend to be adventurous, versatile, freedom-loving, and curious.

6: Individuals born on the 6th of the month possess pure Venus energy and tend to be nurturing, responsible, compassionate, and family-oriented.

7: Individuals born on the 7th of the month possess pure Ketu/Neptune energy and tend to be analytical, intellectual, introspective, and spiritual.

8: Individuals born on the 8th of the month possess pure Saturn energy and tend to be ambitious, driven, authoritative, and powerful.

9: Individuals born on the 9th of the month possess pure Mars energy and tend to be humanitarian, compassionate, selfless, and idealistic.

10: Individuals born on the 10th of the month are symbolised by the "Wheel of Fortune" and possess characteristics of honor, faith, and self-confidence. As the 1's energy depletes due to the presence of 0, those born on this day exhibit reduced Sun energy. They are known to be resourceful, determined, confident, and independent.

11: Individuals born on the 11th of the month may experience a somewhat negative influence of the Sun's energy, amplified by the repeated 1, but they also receive the support of the Moon's energy.

12: Individuals born on the 12th of the month receive a mixed outcome of the energies of 1, 2, and 3, with 1 dominating 2. The symbolism associated with this number includes suffering and anxiety of the mind.

13: Individuals born on the 13th of the month receive a mixed outcome of energies from the numbers 1, 3, and 4, with 1 being dominant while 3's energy depletes. In some ancient writings, it is said that those who understand the number 13 will be given power.

14: Individuals born on the 14th of the month receive a mixed outcome of energies from the numbers 1, 4, and 5, with 1 being dominant while 4's energy depletes. These individuals tend to be adventurous, courageous, adaptable, and always willing to try new and different things.

15: Those born on the 15th day of the month receive a mixed outcome of energies from the numbers 1, 5, and 6, with 1 being dominant while 5's energy depletes. They tend to be loyal and creative, with a special inclination towards music.

16: Individuals born on the 16th day of the month receive a mixed outcome of energies from the numbers 1, 6, and 7, with 1 being dominant while 6's energy depletes. They may find it difficult to express their thoughts and feelings.

17: Those born on the 17th day of the month receive a mixed outcome of energies from the numbers 1, 7, and 8, with 1 being dominant while 7's energy depletes. Individuals born on this day tend to be good with money and finances.

18: Individuals born on the 18th day of the month receive a mixed outcome of energies from the numbers 1, 8, and 9, with 1 being dominant while 8's energy depletes. They tend to be good administrators and humanitarian.

19: Individuals born on the 19th day of the month receive a mixed outcome of energies from the numbers 1, 9, and 1, with 1 being dominant while 9's energy depletes. They are versatile prefer to work without any interference.

20: Individuals born on the 20th day of the month are Cooperation, sensitivity, diplomacy, intuition, but because of the 0's presence the 2's good quality depletes.

21: Individuals born on the 21st day of the month receive a mixed outcome of energies from the numbers 2, 1, and 3, with 2 being dominant while 1's energy depletes. They are creative and expressive individuals who possess an optimistic outlook on life.

22: Individuals born on the 22nd day of the month receive a mixed outcome of energies from the numbers 2 and 4, repeated 2 amplified Moon's moodiness . They are hardworking and practical, with excellent organisational skills.

23: Individuals born on the 23rd day of the month receive a mixed outcome of energies from the numbers 2, 3 and 5, with 2 being dominant while 3's energy depletes. They are naturally curious and adventurous, with a love for exploring new things and experiences.

24: People born on the 24th of the month are nurturing, responsible, and compassionate. They receive a mixed outcome of energies from the numbers 2, 4, and 6, with 2 being dominant while 4's energy depletes. They are often motivated and enthusiastic.

25: Individuals born on the 25th of any month are believed to inherit a combination of energies from the numbers 2, 5, and 7. While the energy of 2 is dominant, the influence of 5 is believed to wane. People born on this day are thought to possess intuition, and gentleness.

26: Those born on the 26th of any month are said to receive a blend of energies from the numbers 2, 6, and 8, with the energy of 2 being the most prominent. Traits such as intuition, gentleness are well visible.

27: Individuals born on the 27th of any month are believed to receive a mixture of energies from the numbers 2, 7, and 9, with the energy of 2 being the strongest influence. People born on these days are often drawn to changes and variety.

28: People born on the 28th of any month are believed to receive a blend of energies from the numbers 2, 8, and 1, with the energy of 2 being the most dominant. Traits such as resourcefulness, independence, and determination are common.

29: Those born on the 29th day of any month are believed to experience a combination of energies from the numbers 2 and 9, as well as the heightened potential of the number 11 (as 2+9=11).

30: Individuals born on the 30th day of any month are often characterized as intelligent, creative, and loving. However, the presence of the number 0 in their birthdate can mitigate some of the negative aspects of the number 3, which is a prominent influence on this day. People born on this day may also exhibit traits such as adaptability, sociability, expression, and versatility.

31: Those born on the 31st day of any month are thought to inherit a mixture of energies from the numbers 3, 1, and 4. Individuals born on this day may start from humble beginnings but have the potential to rise steadily through the ranks. Traits such as transformative abilities, regeneration, change, and upheaval may be associated with them.

Numbers, and Zodiac signs

Each of the twelve zodiac signs has a key number linked to it, which you can find in the table. The planets connected to this Zodiac Number strongly shape your personality. Sometimes, this number aligns well with your Life Path Number, and sometimes it doesn't. This difference can impact whether life feels smooth or challenging for you. You might want to consider this number when choosing lucky lottery numbers or seeing if it matches with your current or future house number. Its planetary influence is just as important as your Life Path Number in these cases.

Note down your Zodiac Number as the second most important number for your numerology analysis after the Life Path number.

Your Sun sign reveal your "needs" and "styles." Think of your Sun Sign as a simple sketch/blue print of your personality. It's just the

starting point. While you can learn a lot about yourself and others from Sun Signs, remember that

they're just one piece of the larger zodiac puzzle. Sun sign indicates the position of the Sun at the time of birth. It reflects whether the sign's energy is outwardly focused and direct (yang), or inwardly focused and subtle (yin).

Astrological signs can also be grouped by their "qualities," which describe their general approach to activity and change. There are three qualities: Cardinal signs mark the beginning of each season and are often associated with initiating new projects or ventures. Fixed signs occur in the middle of each season and are known for their stability and consistency. Mutable signs appear as seasons transition, indicating flexibility and adaptability.

Zodiac Sign	Date Range
ARIES	March 21 - April 19
TAURUS	April 20 - May 20
GEMINI	May 21 - June 21
CANCER	June 22 - July 22
LEO	July 23 - August 22
VIRGO	August 23 - September 22

Zodiac Sign	Date Range
LIBRA	September 23 - October 23
SCORPIO	October 24 - November 21
SAGITTARIUS	November 22 - December 21
CAPRICORN	December 22 - January 19
AQUARIUS	January 20 - February 18
PISCES	February 18 - March 20

ZODIAC	PLANET	PLANETARY INFLUENCE
ARIES	MARS	9 (NINE)
TAURUS	VENUS	6 (SIX)
GEMINI	MERCURY	5 (FIVE)
CANCER	MOON	2 (TWO)
LEO	SUN	1 (ONE)
VIRGO	MERCURY	5 (FIVE)
LIBRA	VENUS	6 (SIX)
SCORPIO	MARS	9 (NINE)
SAGITTARIUS	JUPITER	3 (THREE)
CAPRICORN	SATURN	8 (EIGHT)
AQUARIUS	SATURN	8 (EIGHT)
PISCES	JUPITER	3 (THREE)

Leo (Jul 23 - Aug 22) - Number 1:

Leo, connected with numerology number 1, embodies new beginnings, leadership, and self-confidence. Individuals under this sign radiate confidence and charisma, emphasising self-expression and creativity. Passion and a flair for drama define their essence. In numerology, number 1 represents pioneers and natural leaders who prioritise independence and self-assurance.

Cancer (June 22-July 22) - Number 2:

Cancer, associated with numerology number 2, symbolises balance, harmony, and partnership. Those born under this sign demonstrate reliability and practicality, valuing stability and security. Patience and a love for comfort shape their character. Number 2, regarded as peaceful, aligns with those who act as peacemakers, emphasising relationships and harmony.

Sagittarius (November 22-December 21) - Number 3:

Sagittarius, a fire sign linked to numerology number 3, represents growth, expansion, and luck. Individuals born under this sign possess an adventurous spirit, optimism, and a great sense of humour. Their love for travel, philosophical insights, and a broad perspective defines them. Number 3 resonates with Sagittarius, reflecting creativity and self-expression.

Pisces (February 19-March 20) - Number 3

Pisces, a water sign, aligns with numerology number 3, symbolising creativity, self-expression, and communication.

Individuals under this sign often display empathy, intuition, and compassion. Their artistic talents and ability to emotionally connect with others define their nature, resonating strongly with the creative energy of number 3.

Gemini (May 21-June 21) - Number 5

Gemini, an air sign linked to numerology number 5, embodies intelligence, versatility, and communication. Intellectual curiosity and a sociable nature characterise those born under this sign. Their adaptability and excellent communication skills align with the dynamic energy of number 5, representing change and freedom, essential for personal growth.

Virgo (August 23-September 22) - Number 5

Virgo, an earth sign associated with numerology number 5, represents analytical thinking, attention to detail, and practicality. Hardworking and perfectionistic tendencies define their approach to life. The adaptable energy of number 5 complements Virgo's pursuit of change and precision, crucial for achieving their goals.

Taurus (April 20-May 20) - Number 6

Taurus, an earth sign linked with numerology number 6, reflects practicality, stability, and a love of comfort. Dependability and a grounded nature highlight their preference for security. The nurturing energy of number 6 resonates with Taurus's emphasis on compassion and emotional well-being.

Libra (September 23-October 23) - Number 6

Libra, an air sign connected with numerology number 6, signifies diplomacy, charm, and a quest for balance and harmony. Mediation skills and a peaceful nature shape their interactions. The harmonious energy of number 6 aligns with Libra's desire to create balanced environments, fostering inner peace.

Capricorn (December 22-January 19) - Number 8

Capricorn, an earth sign ruled by Saturn, aligns with numerology number 8, representing discipline, responsibility, and ambition. A strong work ethic and leadership qualities define their character. Saturn's influence fosters a deep sense of duty and a drive for success, resonating with the structured energy of number 8.

Aquarius (January 20-February 18) - Number 8

Aquarius, an air sign under Saturn's influence, connects with numerology number 8, symbolising independence, innovation, and humanitarianism. Intellectual and unconventional tendencies shape their desire to create positive change. Saturn's disciplined energy supports Aquarius's quest for stability through personal freedom and autonomy.

Aries (March 21-April 19) - Number 9

Aries, a fire sign associated with Mars, resonates with numerology number 9, reflecting energy, passion, and action.

Courage and competitiveness are key traits. Mars's influence on Aries emphasises a bold character, a drive for excitement, and a longing for independence, aligning with the assertive energy of number 9.

Scorpio (October 24-November 21) - Number 9

Scorpio, a water sign also ruled by Mars, aligns with numerology number 9, symbolising intensity, transformation, and emotional depth. A mysterious and powerful nature drives their pursuit of truth. The transformative energy of number 9 complements Scorpio's desire for control, rebirth, and the willingness to take risks to achieve their goals

Personality Number

Adding and reducing the day of birth calculates a person's

Calculating Personality Number		
Birthday	Formula	Single Digit
10 JUL	1 + 0	1
16 JAN	1 + 6	7
29 JUN	2 + 9 = 11 = 11	11/2

personality number. In some books, or resources, an online search engine refers to Personality, Psychic, Birthday, Driver, Mul-ank, or Primary number.

As she started reading, the book explained that each person holds personality number, which is calculated using their birthdate, and Life Path number calculated by adding and reducing all the digits from the complete birth details MM/DD/YYYY Olivia noted that her life path number was 7, while Ethan's was 5.

P1 (1st, 10th, 19th, or 28th)

The planet SUN controls the personality number ONE (1), and the person with personality number (1) desires to become a superior leader, manager who is self-ruling, ambitious, and creative and not scared to take risks remarkable in the throng. Sun-ruled personalities always fixate on their goals and ideas, appearing kind, royal, disciplined, authoritative, strong, original, and kinglike.

They exude confidence and prefer an uninterrupted commute to work. Taking control and leading others brings them joy, and they thrive when free to implement their own ideas. Observing others also adds to their satisfaction.

They want to be on top to start a different activity or task. These people are best suited for politics and higher-level organisational positions since they are skilled at making friends and socialising.

POSITIVE: Independent, Creative, Leaders, Creators

NEGATIVE: Egoistic, Arrogant, Domineering, Anger

P2 (2nd, 11th, 20th, or 29th)

A personality number TWO (2), guided by the MOON, influences the mind. This number reflects someone who excels in team settings and prefers working behind the scenes. Sensitivity, thoughtfulness, and a communal attitude characterise them. Moon-ruled individuals often display a queenly grace, charm, and a delicate nature, which endows them with tenderness, artistic inclinations, and a romantic character.

They project a sense of peace and gentleness. Their imaginative nature fuels creativity, though they may lack determination and struggle to implement their ideas assertively. Often seen as deeply emotional, compassionate, and nurturing, they possess an intuitive ability to understand others' feelings and maintain a strong connection to their family and home.

POSITIVE: Duality, Peaceful, Co-operative, Builder

NEGATIVE: Nagging, Fault-finding, Worried, Susceptible

P3 (3rd, 12th, 21st or 30th)

The planet JUPITER represents the personality number THREE (3). Individuals born with this number are known for their originality, energy, friendliness, and a touch of humour. Jupiter's influence imparts a spiritual, counselling, and independent nature. They are bold, active, dependable, and hardworking, driven by a strong ambition to excel in their field. Their goal is to leave a lasting legacy and be remembered by future generations.

Their forward-looking mindset contributes to their drive and attractiveness. With exceptional conversational skills, they often talk their way to the top. Their interactions are marked by cheerfulness, outgoingness, animation, expressiveness, imagination, and creativity.

POSITIVE: Joyous, Cheerful, Expressional, Comport

NEGATIVE: Sensual, Selfish, Scattering, Impatient

P4 (4th, 13th, 22nd or 31st)

The planet RAHU/URANUS stands for the character number FOUR (4). An individual with the birthday figure 4 is usually sensible, reliable, industrious, honest, equitable, and self-controlled. Personality 4 persons are rebellious, impulsive, irritable, and secretive. Rahu and Ketu, the Moon's two nodes, reflect man's underlying bipolar character. They do not exist as physical entities in the same way that the other seven planets do. They each indicate a point where the Moon's orbit around our planet crosses with the ecliptic of the zodiac constellation.

They view everything from a totally unique angle, who view everything from the same angle. In every disagreement, they argue from the opposing side, and as a result, they amass many secret opponents. They despise laws, legal frameworks and seek to destroy. They always oppose the king and build their own kingdoms.

POSITIVE: Builders, Materialistic, Intellectual, Analytical

NEGATIVE: Critical, Self-limited, Economical, Low-spirited

P5 (5th, 14th, or 23rd)

The planet MERCURY represents the personality number FIVE (5). Those with this number are adventurous and thrive in dynamic environments. Individuals born on the 5th are often magnetic and attract the opposite sex.

Mercury-ruled people are known for their royal, entertaining, cunning, astute, and sensitive nature. As the smallest planet in our solar system, Mercury symbolises quick responses, a changeable personality, sharp wit, and restlessness. Known as an evergreen planet, it represents youthfulness. Despite their inconsistency, they are savvy and sharp, gravitating toward opportunities for quick financial gains and avoiding risky, arduous paths. They make swift decisions and adapt rapidly to new situations.

POSITIVE: Smart, Adaptable, Learned, Resilient, Analytical, Attractive to opposite sex

NEGATIVE: Greediness, Money-minded, Calculative, Careless, Restless, Impulsive

P6 (6th, 15th, or 24th)

The planet VENUS represents the personality number SIX (6). Individuals with this number are artistic and idealistic, finding joy in comforting and nurturing others. They have strong familial bonds, a responsible nature, and a deep affection for children and animals.

Those born under Venus exhibit traits such as amorousness, sensuality, sweetness, diplomacy, and passion. They seek harmony and love in their relationships, offering understanding, stability, trust, and loyalty. Known for their youthful spirit, kindness, eloquence, and refined taste, they are easily attracted to the opposite sex and often receive admiration and respect.

POSITIVE: Guardians, Homely, Luxury, Friendly, Musical

NEGATIVE: Anxious, Self-esteem, Care Seeker, Involvement in the affairs of others, Argues, Domestic or sexual exploitation

P7 (7th, 16th or 25th)

The planet KETU/NEPTUNE is the personality number SEVEN (7). A person with the birthday number 7 is analytical in their decision making, as well as private and caring. Ketu controls those who are mystical, dreamy, intuitive, innovative, and thirsty for true knowledge.

It gives intellect, discriminating power, and psychic powers to its inhabitants. Ketu natives are vocal; they enjoy conversations avoid disputes. They live in their fantasies, are intuitive and inventive, and enjoy exaggerating. In their interactions with others, they are quiet and secretive. Individuals ruled by numerology number 7 are often associated with being introspective, analytical, spiritual, and possessing a deep desire for knowledge and understanding of the world around them.

POSITIVE: Wisdom, Research, Knowledge, Spiritual, Dignified, Educator, Intuitive, Nature lover

NEGATIVE: Distant, Restless, Stubborn, Opinionated, Unpredictable, Skeptical, Unapproachable

P8 (8th, 17th or 26th)

The planet SATURN represents the personality number EIGHT (8). Individuals with this number possess wisdom in managing money, judgment, and large projects. Their ambition, confidence, and authority drive them.

Born under Saturn, they exhibit traits such as wisdom, sincerity, honesty, and a strong sense of justice. They are known for their leadership, organisational skills, and long-lasting impact. While they face challenges and mental suffering from misunderstandings, they turn to spirituality for balance. This number influences their approach to both material and spiritual aspects of life, embodying themes of revolution, determination, and uniqueness.

POSITIVE: Spiritual, Material things, Large executive, Diplomat

NEGATIVE: Power demonstration, Unappreciative, Merciless driver

P9 (9th, 18th or 27th)

The planet MARS governs the personality number NINE (9). Individuals with this number display generosity, open-mindedness, sensitivity, and creativity, often offering unique solutions to problems. This number is closely linked with humanitarianism.

Mars-ruled people are known for their strength, assertiveness, and perfectionism. They possess a strong will and determination, allowing them to make significant progress in their pursuits. They respond swiftly to challenges and remain vigilant at the first sign of trouble. While ambitious and driven, they may face financial or personal conflicts, never submitting to others' control.

They are brave and make excellent soldiers. Their self-love is the primary source of their adversity. They dislike receiving counsel. They enjoy being powerful in their personal lives.

POSITIVE: Humanitarian, Action driven, Artistic, Sympathy

NEGATIVE: Selfish, Miserly, Destructive, Anger

Life Path Number

Life path number derived through adding the digits of the birth date, month, and year until we obtain a single digit number. If the total comes to 11 or 22, we stop further reducing and write as 11/2, 22/4.

STEP1		
DD	MM	YYYY
21	10	1981

STEP2 (Addition)
2+1+1+1+9+8+1 = 23

STEP3 (Reduce)
2+3 = 5

STEP2 (Add Digits)	
MONTH	10
DAY	21
YEAR	1981
TOTAL	2012

STEP3 (Reduce)
2+1+2 = 5

The life path number known as Destiny, Conductor, and Bhagya Ank number.

The life path number is one of the most important numerological calculations, as it provides a blueprint for a person's journey through life. This number is often seen as a guide or a map that helps individuals navigate the ups and downs of life, make better choices, and discover their true potential. It is also believed that each life path number has its own unique set of challenges and opportunities, and understanding these help people make the most of their lives.

The life number becomes active between the ages of 27 and 30 and it shows the purpose of an individual's life. The number shows that one has to work for the level of self- development. We consider eleven life path numbers: 1, 2, 3, 4, 5, 6, 7, 8, 9, 11, and 22, Eleven and Twenty-two known as master number and bring in added energy and spiritual awareness.

Life Path Calculation: A man born on Oct 21, 1981.

The Life-path number is FIVE (5) for Oct 21, 1981

Special Note: If you arrive to either 11 or 22 at the step2, please confirm if it's a master number as below:

- January =1, February = 2, March = 3, April = 4, May = 5, June = 6, July = 7, August = 08, September = 09, October = 10, November = 11, and December = 12

  - Add all the digits together and finally reduce to a single digit

  - If the calculated number become either 11 or 22, please refer the special note.Life Path awakens the individual's specific interests, unique abilities, attitudes, talents, and guides him to the purpose of one's being on Earth.

1 Life Path

ONE: The Leader

Lesson: to overcome obstacles by personal creativity.

Path: originality, independence, concentration, confidence, perception, efficiency.

Goal: to express individuality and lead the way for others to follow.

Independence is the perfect word to describe the 1 life path number. People with the life path number 1 must learn to stand independent and meet their goals. They may appear dependent until the age of 27-30, but they become independent and remain pioneers in the latter half of their lives. As they grow, they become trend-makers, originators, and influencers in the end.

2 Life Path

TWO: The Sensitive

Lesson: To be able to give and take when collaborating with others.

Path: Tact, Diplomacy, Gregarity, Consideration, Patience, Purgation, Friendliness.

Goal: To be able to work as a member of a team.

Collaboration, harmony, and serenity depict the number Two.

Those born along the journey of life (2) are cooperative, helpful, modest, neat, tactful, and diplomatic.

People with a two destiny number puts others at ease. They appear cordial and charming, and they make excellent hosts and hostesses. They are sensitive and make new friends. They would rather be in a long-term relationship than be alone. By nature, they are gentle, peaceful, and perceptive. They set up good friends and communicate. They are unconcerned their social standing or material demands.

As a result, they usually find themselves as the secondary leader builder rather than the leader.

3 Life Path

THREE: The Versatile

Lesson: To be able to express yourself freely.

Path: self-development, taking opportunities as they arise, convivial surroundings, working alone.

Goal: To achieve success and personal freedom through the development of your innate creative talents.

The word self-expression best describes 3 life path number. Creativity, optimism, inspiration, and a want to live to the fullest depict a Life Path 3 person. As a result, they drew to occupations in writing, speaking, singing, acting, or teaching. Those with the number 3 must express themselves. Because this manifestation involves verbal abilities, it might encompass singing, talking, or writing. Threes are superb conversationalists, and their strength is communication. They have lively, imaginative brains that are buzzing with ideas. But, they lack the motivation to put them to use. They place a high emphasis on friendships; as a result, they stay loyal to friends. Because of the social spirit of 3, Jupiter is the governing planet. These individuals are cheerful, humorous the entertainer, enthusiastic, skilled at writing, speaking, and singing, prefer to be happier, enjoy children, and are self-expressive.

4 Life Path

FOUR: The Builder

Lesson: To be responsible for your actions.

Path:Be prepared to work hard, pay attention to detail, don't take unnecessary risks, be patient, learn from your mistakes, be efficient, practice thrift, never give up but learn to accept reality.

Goal: To lay down solid foundations on which to build your life, to be practical and good organiser.

The word practice, order, and routine best describes 4 life path number.

People with a life path number of 4 must work hard. They are realistic, dependable, attentive, and well-organised individuals who appreciate following routines. They bring order out of chaos. The workers take pleasure in seeing the fruits of their labor. Fours will trudge along for years if they see that the work is worthwhile. They are detail-oriented and like fine, complex work. They are stiff and stubborn people who find it difficult to change their ideas after they have made up their minds.

These individuals display discipline, family orientation, hard work, honesty, organisation, patience, patriotism, practicality, and dependability.

4 corresponds to the demand for order, service, and management. This, along with a good dose of patience and thoroughness, makes them ideal for a job in construction, engineering, and handicraft, as well as any industry that values planning, organising, regulating, and following a routing.

5 Life Path

FIVE: The Adventurer

Lesson: To discover the right way to use freedom.

Path: Be progressive, keep up with new ides and tackle problems with ingenuity, shun monotony and don't get bogged down, learn through travel and personal experience, use money wisely, experience as much possible of life, seek variety.

Goal: To value freedom and realise that nothing in life in permanent.

The words liberty, experience, and movement best describe 5 life path number.

They are Versatile, Bold, Engaging, Intelligent, Independent, Sociable, Great marketers, Wry, Globetrotters, drawn to physical attraction, liberty, seeks progress, and leads an equilibrium lifestyle are qualities of individuals born under the sign of Five (5). We consider the 5 a harmonious, magical number;

They are likely to explore early in life, but once they discover their actual course, they accomplish a great deal. These people are always inquisitive, enthusiastic, and young at heart.

Multi-talented and adaptive nature comes with the life figure 5, as the ruling planet Mercury shows vitality on those people. As a result, they posses ability to perform multiple things at the same time.

Overindulgence is a bad for them. These people change their minds and find it difficult to commit to anything for an extended period. Many people experiment with and abuse alcohol, drugs, and sex.

6 Life Path

SIX: The Peacemaker

Lesson: To be responsible for members of your family and the community.

Path: Be responsible to the social needs of others, show compassion and understanding, be loving and bring comfort, show sympathy when needed and try to equalise injustices through your own good judgement.

Goal: To be of service to others and give help and support when it is called for.

The words luxury, home, and family best describe 6 life path number.

Individuals with the life path number 6 are nurturing, kind, and responsible. They appreciate bearing other people's troubles and lending a shoulder to others. They take great pleasure in assisting those they care.

When things are not going well, they become family members. Sixes make sure that everyone is satisfied with the outcome of interpersonal conflicts. Their friends and loved ones surround them and make them happier. They are sympathetic and kind. Sixes are inventive, especially in the arts. People with this number are more likely to be artistic, domestic, humanitarian, musical, nurturing, responsible, serving, and teachers.

This life path strives for responsibility, love, balance, helpful, conscientious, and capable of resolving a controversial issue. These qualities make the the life path number 6 ideal for occupations working with the elderly, young, sick, and poor.

7 Life Path

SEVEN: The Mysterious

Lesson: To develop the mind in order to gain wisdom and understanding.

Path: You must study, learn, search for truth, try to find the answers to life's problems, when you speak make sure you say something worth listening to, spend time your own (this is essential for inner growth), study the past and the occult, read, think and meditate.

Goal: To be able to use your wisdom and knowledge to guide others.

Research, education, and analysis are the words describes the 7 life path number.

Individuals with a life path number of 7 require solitude to increase their understanding and skill. They take a distinct, one-of-a-kind approach to everything they carry out. This gives them originality, but it makes it difficult for them to evolve and adapt. It makes it hard for them to settle in a group setting.

Sevens prefer smaller circles of friends to giant circles of friends. They   be challenging to comprehend at first because they secure themselves with defences, but they make wonderful friends once they trust the other person.

Life path number is associated with introspective, solitary, dignified, educator, intuitive, nature lover, silent, spiritual or scientific, and studious.

They are drawn to activities that require thought and study. They are deep thinkers, withdrawn, and aloof. They are also believed to be specialists in the field they specialise in.

Those with a 7 have a preference for working alone at their own pace, and they have difficulty expressing - or understanding their emotions. Perfectionists are sensible people who apply logic to everything they do.

People on the negative side of their 7 life path find it difficult connecting others so prefer to isolate themselves. They become more self-centred and introverted.

8 Life Path

EIGHT: The Materialist

Lesson: To stay successful in the material world with authority.

Path: Hard work, organisation, sound judgement, use your energy constructively and work towards a specific goal, be ambitious, learn poise, assurance and self-control.

Goal: To demonstrate success and leadership through example.

8 life path number is best described by the terms materialism, judgement, and efficiency.

Individuals with the life path number 8 enjoy large-scale enterprises and seek to help from their success. They set high standards for themselves and strive hard to carry out them. They are determined and ambitious, and they always succeed. We ground eights in reality and do not have time to daydream.

8s are ambitious, athletic, and efficient, with executive skills, sound judgement, and stamina.

This life path is associated with material wealth and financial security, as well as great project planning, initiation, and completion talents. It is important not to misinterpret this determination as intransigence or avarice.

They are often natural leaders who are not afraid of taking risks or making difficult decisions. However, the influence of Saturn also make them cautious and pragmatic, which means they tend to approach their endeavours in a methodical and deliberate manner. If they navigate in undesirable activities, they may make wealth, but at the expense of their health, happiness, and relationships. They have the potential to become intolerant, spiteful, and power-hungry.

9 Life Path

NINE: The Visionary

Lesson: To develop a broadminded attitude to life.

Path: To be of service to others, show compassion and understanding, cultivate a working knowledge of world affairs, learn to live up to your ideals, be patient, don't give half way through a project, do as you would be done by.

Goal: To show others the right way to live through your breadth of thinking and try to promote universal love and harmony.

Humanitarianism, selflessness, and understanding are the best words to describe the 9 life path number.

People with the life path number 9 prone to self-sacrifice. They are sensitive, loving individuals who have a strong desire to serve assisting others and give rather than receive. As a result, they are exploitable, devastated when their deep and sincere love was not returned.

People with the life path number nine (9) exhibit artistic abilities, brotherly love, compassion, drama, philanthropy, and selflessness. This number is associated with compassion, good deeds, and awareness of others' needs. As a result, someone with this number must be eager to work hard and to encourage others. People with this number are innovative, creative, artistic, and they love their friendships.

Those with Life Path number 9 must use extreme caution to avoid being selfish or self-entered, which might occur if their personal objectives take precedence over those of the greater good.

They have a strong sense of justice and a desire to make a positive impact on the world. The influence of Mars makes them assertive and independent. However, they must stay careful and maintain their aggression.

Name Numerology

In Chaldean name numerology, we assign each letter a specific number value based on its sound vibration. These values range from 1 to 8.

A name numerologist analyses the numerical values of a person's name to offer insights into their strengths, weaknesses, and potential for success. Name numerology select a name for a newborn, choose a new name for oneself or a business, personal growth and self-awareness. With knowledge of the Chaldean

1	2	3	4	5	6	7	8
A	B	C	D	E	U	O	F
I	K	G	M	H	V	Z	P
J	R	L	T	N	W		
Q		S		X			
Y							

chart, letters, and specific number associations, one understand and apply name numerology.

Chaldean Name Numerology

In this example we would find the name numerology number using the above table for:

CHALDEAN NUMEROLOGY To decide an individual's numerological value, we use their full name, as the letters in their name holds specific vibrations. The process assigns each letter in the name a numerical value based on the above table, and then adds these values together to create a single-digit number, or a master number.

One of the most common usage of this technique is to transform a person's birth name into a number.

Numerology number compatibility is the practice of analysing the compatibility between two individuals based on their numerological values. Each number holds a specific vibration

C	H	A	L	D	E	A	N
3	5	1	3	4	5	1	5

N	U	M	E	R	O	L	O	G	Y
5	6	4	5	2	7	3	7	3	1

STEP 1		
FIRST NAME	REDUCING	DIGIT
35134515	3 + 5 + 1 + 3 + 4 + 5 + 1 + 5	27
		9

STEP 2		
LAST NAME	REDUCING	DIGIT
5645273731	5 + 6 + 4 + 5 + 2 + 7 + 3 + 7 + 3 + 1	43
		7

STEP 3		
DIGITS	REDUCING	DIGIT
9,7	9 + 7	16
		7

and energy, hence used to determine an individual's personality traits, tendencies, and life path.

Certain numbers appears compatible with each other, while others may conflict or incompatible. Numerology number compatibility helps individuals gain insight into various aspects of a relationship, such as compatibility, communication, and emotional bonding.

Understanding each other's numerological values and energies fosters stronger, more fulfilling relationships and helps in achieving shared goals. Every individual has an aura–a field of energy that aligns their emotions, thoughts, and body. Those who have mastered balancing their aura often find greater success, improved relationships, and increased happiness.

This concept is reflected in the allies, neutrals, and adversaries chart in numerology. This chart guides through various areas of a life, such as career, business, and relationships. By balancing and expanding your aura, you attract positive elements into your life. An aura surrounds all things on earth, and when you resonate harmoniously, you attract beneficial outcomes.

1 and 2 form a compatible pairing due to their complementary qualities. Number 1 brings leadership, ambition, and determination, while number 2 offers supportive and nurturing qualities, providing emotional backing and understanding. Their partnership balances ambition with emotional depth, fostering harmony.

2 and 7 share a profound connection through their emotional and spiritual understanding. Number 2 seeks harmony and is sensitive, while number 7 is introspective and spiritual. This alignment allows them to connect deeply on both emotional and spiritual levels.

3 and 5 make a compatible match, both being adventurous and creative. Number 3 is expressive and sociable, whereas number 5 is curious and adaptable. Their shared love for new experiences and creativity makes their relationship dynamic and exciting.

4 and 8 align well due to their shared focus on practicality and business success. Number 4 is grounded and diligent, while number 8 emphasises achievement and authority. Together, they build a stable and prosperous life, combining their strengths in a compatible partnership.

5 and 9 resonate well with each other as they both value freedom and independence. Number 5 is adventurous and flexible, while number 9 is compassionate and idealistic. Their relationship supports personal growth and individual dreams, making it harmonious.

6 and 2 are compatible through their mutual nurturing and supportive nature. Number 6, being family-oriented and caring, complements number 2's emotional support and understanding. Their combined qualities create a loving and harmonious home life.

7 and 9 connect through their shared spiritual and intellectual pursuits. Number 7, analytical and introspective, aligns with number 9's compassion and idealism. Their relationship is enriched by exploring philosophical and spiritual matters together.

8 and 1 form a strong partnership due to their shared drive for success and leadership. Number 8's ambition and practicality

align with number 1's leadership qualities. Together, they work towards achieving their goals and creating a powerful, influential alliance.

In numerology, the influence of numbers such as 8, 3, 6, and 9 can play a significant role in various aspects of life, including marriage. According to numerological beliefs, these numbers can indicate patterns or tendencies that might affect one's journey to marriage or the timing of it. To understand these influences, one must analyse their birthdate by breaking it down into single digits for the day, month, and year of birth.

Here are a few examples to illustrate the point:

1. 17-11-1990:

    - Day (1+7=8)

    - Month (1+1=2)

    - Year (1+9+9+0=19, 1+9=10, 1+0=1)

2. 9-3-2006:

    - Day (9)

    - Month (3)

    - Year (2+0+0+6=8)

3. 27-5-1983:

    - Day (2+7=9)

    - Month (5)

-         Year (1+9+8+3=21, 2+1=3)

4. 6-12-1969:

-         Day (6)

-         Month (1+2=3)

-         Year (1+9+6+9=25, 2+5=7)

In these birthdates, noticed a combination of numbers 8, 3, 6, and 9. At least two of these numbers are present in each birthdate, and this combination is believed to lead to difficulties in marriage. Such individuals might experience delays in getting married, and even after marriage, they may encounter marital problems. This observation is said to hold true in approximately 60% to 70% of cases.

Let's delve into specific numbers that are considered unfavourable for marriage:

Number 4: dates that add up to the number 4, such as the 4th, 13th, 22nd, or 31st of any month, or where the sum of the day, month, and year equals 4, are thought to be associated with financial difficulties and relationship complexities. It's believed that marriages occurring on these dates might encounter financial struggles and various marital challenges.

However, it's crucial to acknowledge that numerology is not universally recognised as a science, and its influence on real-life events like marriage is largely a matter of personal belief. Interpretations of numerology can vary based on cultural and regional perspectives. While some individuals may consider these numerical associations when planning significant life events, others might not place any importance on them.

Ultimately, the success of a marriage is influenced by numerous factors beyond numerological considerations, including love, compatibility, communication, and mutual understanding.

Number 5: marriage dates that involve the number 5–such as the 5th, 14th, 23rd, or any date where the sum of the day, month, and year reduces to 5–are thought to bring unique challenges to couples. These challenges may include misunderstandings, ego-driven arguments, and, in some cases, the possibility of divorce.

It's important to remember that numerology's influence on real-life events like marriage is based on personal belief rather than empirical evidence. Interpretations can vary by culture and region. While some may consider these numerical associations when choosing a marriage date, the success of a marriage ultimately depends on factors such as communication, mutual respect, and understanding.

Choosing marriage dates with the number 5, such as the 5th, 14th, or 23rd, is believed to bring challenges due to the number's associations with change, unpredictability, and a strong desire for freedom. While these traits can be positive, they might create discord and instability in the marriage.

Here's a more detailed breakdown of how the number 5 affects a marriage:

Choosing dates with the number 5, such as the 5th, 14th, or 23rd, may lead to:

- **Misunderstandings:** Increased miscommunications and disputes over important matters.

- **Egoistic Arguments:** Conflicts arising from strong individualism and personal priorities.

- **Divorce:** If unresolved, these challenges may strain the marriage, potentially leading to divorce.

Remember, numerology's influence on life events, including marriage, is subjective. While some consider these aspects when choosing dates, others focus on factors like love, communication, and compatibility for a successful marriage.

Choosing dates like the 8th, 17th, or 26th, or those that sum to 8, might introduce challenges in a relationship. Avoiding these dates could lead to a more harmonious marriage. While numerology offers insights, successful marriages depend on communication, mutual respect, and compatibility.

Based on my experience and research, couples with harmonising birth numbers often enjoy more loving and harmonious marriages. In contrast, mismatched vibrational energies can lead to difficulties. I recommend seeking a numerological compatible partner and avoiding the previously mentioned marriage dates for a smoother relationship.

Here are a few basic guidelines for specific birth numbers:

Birth Number 1 (those born on 1, 10, 19, and 28)

If you belong to this category, you have a natural inclination toward marriage, but finding a compatible partner becomes challenging. You drawn to intellectual types, which may result in a lack of emotional warmth in your relationships. To enhance compatibility, consider selecting a partner born during specific periods and governed by numbers 2, 3, or 9.

You often find success on dates like the 1st, 10th, 19th, and 28th for your creative plans. You tend to be very friendly with individuals born on dates associated with numbers 2, 4, and 7, such as the 2nd, 4th, 7th, 11th, 13th, 16th, 20th, 22nd, 25th, 29th, and 31st. Sundays and Mondays are particularly auspicious for you; aligning these dates with the mentioned numbers can lead to highly fruitful outcomes.

You have a natural inclination towards marriage and appreciate a partner who shares your enthusiasm for life and has an eye for beauty and style, both privately and publicly. However, finding a companion who perfectly aligns with your preferences can be challenging, leading to occasional disappointment in your married life. While you are often drawn to intellectual types, this preference can sometimes create a gap in passion and emotional warmth, despite your own intellectual pursuits. As a result, achieving the desired balance in your relationship may require extra effort.

You appreciate a partner who shares your enthusiasm for life and values both inner and outer beauty, whether at home or in public. However, finding someone who aligns perfectly with these preferences can be challenging, which might lead to occasional disappointment in your married life. While you are often drawn to intellectual types, this focus on intellect can sometimes create a gap in passion and emotional warmth, despite your own intellectual pursuits. Achieving balance in your relationship may require extra effort.

You have an inherent attraction to individuals born within the specified date ranges: July 21 to August 20 (Leo), November 21 to December 20 (Sagittarius), and March 21 to April 20 (Aries). Reflecting on prospective partners from these time frames could enhance compatibility and contribute to a harmonious and fulfilling marriage.

Birth Number 2 (those born on 2, 11, 20, and 29)

For you, with a number 2 birth, your inherent nature is nurturing and emotionally sensitive, often valuing deep connections over fiery passions. You might find yourself drawn to partners with significant age differences, appreciating the wisdom and life experience they bring. Your intuitive abilities are finely tuned when it comes to matters of the heart and marriage complexities.

You naturally gravitate toward individuals born between November 23 and December 21 (Sagittarius) and February 19 to March 20 (Pisces). Therefore, it's advisable to consider choosing your life partner from these date ranges, associated with the

Zodiac signs Sagittarius and Pisces. You also share a strong connection with those influenced by the numbers 2, 4, and 6.

According to numerology, if your birth number is 2, your ideal match would be someone with a birth number of 1, 3, or 7. There's a mutual attraction between you and those with birth number 7, which can lead to a highly successful and harmonious marriage. Marrying someone with birth number 7 brings adoration, worship, and success into your life. Compatibility also extends to those with birth numbers 3 and 6, promising a happy married life with supportive partners. However, exercise caution with individuals born on the 6th, 15th, and 24th, especially if they have a strong desire for material success.

Numerology suggests that those with Personality number 2 should avoid marriage with individuals bearing personality number 1. Personality 1 individuals tend to be practical and less emotionally driven, which may result in shorter-lived love and a propensity for dominance. It's essential to be cautious of any quarrelsome or controlling behaviour when considering a marriage partner with Personality number 1.

Birth Number 3 (those born on 3, 12, 21, and 30)

As a person with a birth number 3, you are naturally drawn to partners born within certain date ranges: July 23 to August 22 (Leo), October 23 to November 21 (Scorpio), and November 22 to December 21 (Sagittarius). It's advisable to consider these periods when choosing your life partner. Additionally, you share a strong affinity with individuals influenced by numbers 3, 2, 6, and 9, so selecting a partner with one of these numbers from the specified date ranges is highly recommended.

Your magnetic pull is strongest with individuals who have birth numbers 1, 2, or 9. You share a deep bond with individuals whose Life Path Number is either 3 or 9. For the most harmonious and peaceful marriage, consider partners born on the 3rd, 12th, 21st, or 30th. When the Life Number of 3 is present, marriage can result in a calm and prosperous relationship.

However, be cautious with individuals who have 9 as their Birth or Life Number, as their high activity and aggression might require you to adopt a more submissive role. Avoid marrying those born on the 8th, 17th, or 26th, as these dates correspond to the number 8, which incompatible with number 3.

In numerology, the number 3 corresponds to Guru or Jupiter, while the number 6 relates to Shukra or Venus–considered adversaries in Hindu mythology. Therefore, marrying someone with the number 6 as their Birth or Life Number should be approached with caution to avoid potential relationship issues.

People born on dates like the 2nd, 11th, 20th, or 29th are compatible partners for you. Whether their Birth or Life number is 2, these unions lead to happiness and the gift of well-behaved children.

If you're thinking about marrying someone with number 4, watch out for incompatibilities. Those who fall under Number 3 appear less talkative, whereas Number 4 individuals are outgoing and spend more money, resulting in potential difficulties in communication and financial habits in marriage.

Birth Number 4 (those born on 4, 13, 22, and 31)

As a person with a birth number 4, you are naturally attracted to individuals whose birthdays fall within specific date ranges. You may find compatibility with those born from May 21 to June 20 (Gemini), August 23 to September 22 (Virgo), and September 23 to October 22 (Libra). For a potentially harmonious relationship, consider choosing a life partner from these time frames. Additionally, you connect well with individuals influenced by numbers 5, 6, and 8.

You drawn to individuals with Birth Numbers 4 or 8, as these partnerships often lead to stability and shared values. Partners with a Life Path Number of 4 or 8 can also contribute to a successful and contented marriage. For optimal compatibility, consider marrying someone born on dates like the 4th, 13th, 22nd, or 31st.

However, it's advisable to avoid marrying individuals born on dates such as the 8th, 17th, or 26th, as these correspond to the number 8, which may present challenges in the relationship. Further, exercise caution when dealing with partners whose Life or Birth Number is 6, as 6 is incompatible with 4.

The number 4 represents structure and stability, the number 3 (Guru or Jupiter) may sometimes create mismatches. Marrying someone with the personality number 3 might require extra effort to address differences in communication and financial habits.

Birth Number 5 (those born on 5, 14, 23)

As a person with a birth number of 5, you naturally seek partners whose birthdays fall within specific date ranges for better compatibility. Your desire for a harmonious relationship mirrors that of individuals with a Birth Number of 1. Like them, you appreciate a partner who shares your enthusiasm for life and has a keen eye for beauty and style, both privately and publicly. However, finding a companion who perfectly aligns with your preferences can be challenging and may lead to occasional disappointment in your married life.

Similar to those with Birth Number 1, you might face difficulties in balancing intellectual pursuits with emotional warmth and passion in your relationship. To enhance compatibility, you may find success with individuals born between May 21 and June 20 (Gemini), August 23 and September 22 (Virgo), and July 23 and August 22 (Leo).

You have a good rapport with people who are affected by the numerological numbers 1, 4, and 6. Because the numbers compliment each other's energy and personalities, marriages with spouses whose birth numbers match 5 or 9 can be very happy and fulfilling.

Birth Number 6 (those born on 6, 15, 24)

As an individual with a birth number of 6, you naturally gravitate towards partners born within specific date ranges that enhance compatibility. Similar to those with Birth Number 1, your tendencies often lead you to seek companions born between April 21 and May 20 (Taurus), September 23 and October 22 (Libra), May 21 and June 20 (Gemini), August 23 and September 22 (Virgo), and October 23 and November 21 (Scorpio). Selecting a partner from these periods can significantly improve your chances of a harmonious relationship.

Your appreciation for both inner and outer beauty and enthusiasm for life aligns with your search for a compatible partner. However, as with Number 1 individuals, finding someone who perfectly matches these preferences can be challenging and may occasionally lead to disappointment.

In addition to these astrological signs, you also connect well with individuals influenced by numerology numbers 4, 5, and 8. Marrying someone with these numbers, especially within the specified date ranges, often leads to a harmonious and fulfilling relationship, as your energies and personalities resonate on a deeper level.

Birth Number 7 (those born on 7, 16, 25)

As an individual with a birth number of 7, your unique charm and depth often lead you to seek partners born within certain date ranges for greater compatibility. Like those with Birth

Number 1, you may find a strong connection with individuals born between March 21 and April 19 (Aries), July 23 and August 22 (Leo), and November 22 and December 21 (Sagittarius). Choosing a partner from these periods can significantly enhance your compatibility.

Your search for emotional depth and a profound connection often mirrors the experiences of Number 1 individuals in their pursuit of intellectual and emotional balance. While your depth of character is captivating, it may also make it challenging to find a partner who fully understands and resonates with your profound insights. This can lead to moments where you seek additional emotional warmth and passion in your relationships.

Additionally, you have a special affinity with individuals influenced by numerology numbers 8, 6, and 5. Selecting a life partner with these numbers from the specified date ranges can often lead to a harmonious and fulfilling marriage, as your energies and personalities complement each other.

Birth Number 8 (those born on 8, 17, 26)

As an individual with a birth number of 8, your natural inclinations often draw you toward people born within certain date ranges, much like how Number 1 individuals are attracted to specific signs. You tend to find compatibility and happiness with those born between September 23 and October 22 (Libra), December 22 and January 19 (Capricorn), and January 20 and February 18 (Aquarius). Choosing a life partner from these periods can significantly enhance your chances of a harmonious relationship.

Your journey towards a fulfilling partnership often revolves around ambition and achievement, reflecting your desire for success and the need for a partner who supports and understands your goals. This focus on ambition can sometimes resemble the challenges faced by Number 1 individuals in balancing intellectual and emotional aspects of their relationships.

You appear sharing a unique connection with individuals influenced by numerology numbers 4, 5, and 6. As advised to Number 1 individuals, opting for a life partner with these numbers from the specified date ranges can lead to a successful and fulfilling marriage, as your energies and ambitions align to create a prosperous partnership.

Birth Number 9 (those born on 9, 18, 27)

As someone with a birth number of 9, you often find yourself naturally drawn to individuals born within specific date ranges when seeking an ideal life partner. Much like how Number 1 individuals seek compatibility with particular signs, you tend to connect well with those born between March 21 and April 19 (Aries), October 23 and November 21 (Scorpio), and November 22 and December 21 (Sagittarius). Marrying a partner from these time frames can significantly enhance your chances of compatibility and happiness.

Your pursuit of depth, spirituality, and inner connection mirrors the quest of Number 1 individuals for intellectual and emotional balance. While you seek a profound spiritual and emotional alignment with your partner, finding someone who resonates deeply with your insights can sometimes be a challenge, similar to the emotional warmth and passion sought by Number 1 individuals.

You resonate with people who are affected by the numbers 1, 2, and 3 in numerology. Similar to 1 people, selecting a life mate with one of these numbers within the designated time frames might cause a happy union as your spiritual goals and energy coincide in significant ways.

It's important to remember that while numerology provides intriguing insights into compatibility, successful and lasting relationships are built on more than just these elements. Communication, respect, shared values, and a deep emotional connection are foundational to any enduring partnership.

In our exploration of numerology, we've uncovered a valuable tool for understanding relationship dynamics. By examining personality, life path, and name numerology, we've gained insights into the unique traits and attributes each person brings to a relationship.

As we end, it's apparent that numerology brings meaningful perspectives to relationship compatibility. Examining personality, life path, and name numerology can help in navigating committed partnerships or marriage. Our personal numerological profiles act as a roadmap, revealing our unique qualities and helping us understand ourselves better. This knowledge enables us to embark on a path of self-improvement, growing to become the best versions of ourselves and cultivating more harmonious relationships.

It's important to recognise that our life path numbers guide us on our personal journeys. We unveil the life lessons we need to learn and the paths we're meant to take. Through understanding our individual life paths and those of our potential partners, we can harmonise our aspirations and objectives, forming a unified roadmap for the future. This awareness enables us to plan for goals, overcome challenges, and flourish as a group.

It is crucial to take into account the significant influence of our names in numerology. Names are more than simple labels. Our names' compatibility with our partners can affect a relationship's energy. It can either enhance or disrupt its flow. By knowing the energy of our names, we can choose our partners. This will ensure their vibrations align positively with ours.

Numerology compatibility is a powerful tool. It reveals the depths of love and partnership. It provides valuable insights to foster understanding and empathy in relationships. With this, we can improve our partnerships. We can build unions based on respect, shared dreams, and aligned energies.

As you plan your wedding, remember this. Numerology is not a crystal ball. It won't offer guarantees. But, it can guide you on your journey together. With this, may your union be filled with love and understanding. May you share a vision for a future that meets your highest hopes. Numerology compatibility can lead to a happy life with your love.

Numerology is a powerful tool for understanding personality and life paths. But it has its limits. Numerology studies the energy of numbers and letters in names and birthdates. It excels at revealing personality traits and compatibility based on them. Yet, it fails to address the complexities of a deeper relationship.

Astrology offers a better view of compatibility. It considers the positions of celestial bodies at birth. Astrology is often seen as better for marriage compatibility. Here are a few key reasons:

1. Astrology looks at the positions of the sun, moon, planets, and other celestial bodies at one's birth. It relates these to a birth chart. These placements create complex interactions. They offer insights into a person's personality, tendencies, and life experiences. In contrast, numerology focuses on simpler numbers from names and birth dates.

2. Time and Occurrences in Life, Astrology is excellent in foretelling the dates of significant life events, such as shifts in career and health problems. It enables astrologers to determine the long-term compatibility of a relationship. They take into account the timing of significant life events that could impact the partnership.

3. Delves into the emotional and psychological aspects of an individual's personality. When figuring out compatibility, it is crucial. It can reveal a person's emotional requirements

and communication style. It may also reveal their coping mechanisms. A relationship's dynamics are altered by several elements. Numerology is too shallow to deal with these complex issues.

4.   Astrology is great at checking the compatibility of two birth charts. Astrologers compare the planets in each person's chart. It shows a relationship's strengths and challenges. Numerology is less specific than this method. It tailors to the individuals involved.

5.   Views individuals as undergoing lifelong transformation and change. It considers the movements of celestial bodies over time. It offers insights into personal growth and its impact on relationships.

Numerology helps with basic compatibility. It uses personality and life paths. Astrology, however, offers a deeper analysis of relationship dynamics. Astrology's deep, evolving view of a person's life and mind makes it a top choice for marriage tests.

Refer the Numerology compatibility chart:

NUMBERS	FRIENDS	NEUTRAL	EMENY
1	2 3 4 5 6 9	1 6 7	8
2	1 2 3 5 7	4 9	6 8
3	1 2 3 5 9	4 7 8	4 6
4	1 5 6 7	2 3 4 8	2 9
5	1 2 4 5 6 8	3 7 9	
6	4 5 6 8	1 2 3 6 7	2 9
7	4 5 6 8	1 2 3 7 9	
8	5 6 7	2 3 4 8 9	1 9
9	1 3 5 7	2 9	4 6 8 9

Chapter 3 : Karmic Numbers

In numerology, Karmic numbers show past-life experiences. They can affect your present and future. These numbers are 10, 13, 14, 16, and 19. Let's take a closer look at each of these Karmic numbers.

A Karmic number in numerology foretells difficult obstacles in your life. Karmic Lessons and Karmic Debts are the two categories of Karmic Numbers. Karmic Lessons are less strong, but Karmic Debts have a bigger effect. Here, we are concentrating on the Karmic Numbers 10, 13, 14, 16, and 19.

Karmic Debts are also known as Testing Numbers, Warning Numbers, or Hidden Numbers. They state that you must settle a karmic account from a previous existence. A Karmic Debt number in your numerology chart means you are struggling with your past.

Let's delve into the essence of each of these Karmic Debt Numbers:

Karmic Debt Number 10/1

The compound number 10 holds similarities to the number 1 but is imbued with added authoritative power and a sense of completeness. The number 10 signifies a spiritual journey of growth and development. It hints the potential to achieve remarkable feats, but this journey may be fraught with challenges. To fulfil your destiny, you may need to release old patterns and beliefs that no longer serves you, clearing the way for progress and personal evolution. The Karmic Debt Number 10 encourages to embrace, change and transformation on the path towards self-realisation and greatness.

Karmic Debt Number 19/1

The number 19/1 embodies wisdom, power, and spiritual knowledge that was previously misused for self-centred personal gain. If this number is among the Core Numbers, it implies to paying the dues for past misuses of sacred knowledge, a lack of compassion, and spiritual misalignment. The 19/1 signifies a substantial abuse of power, and calculated selfish actions. Individuals with this number exhibits destructive traits as narcissism, egotism, selfishness, dependence, and a lack of self-confidence. Overcoming these traits and mastering the associated lessons is essential.

Karmic Debt Number 13/4

The 13/4 carries the essence of creative energy and joy that devolved into superficiality and hurtful words in a prior life. If this number is the Core Numbers, it signifies a need to make amends for past abuses where the fair distribution of workload neglected. The 13, often considered an "unlucky" number, indicates hard work and balance. It urges to master the art of positive expression, exercise discipline in practical matters, and avoid blame-shifting, bossiness, and rigidity. The 13/4 calls for responsible and considerate communication.

Karmic Debt Number 14/5

The number 4 in the 14/5 denotes the misuse of freedom in a past life, where personal freedom pursued at the expense of others. This Karmic Debt emphasises irresponsibility and an inclination towards excessive behaviours. The number 5 signifies the need for constructive freedom through self-discipline. Those with the 14/5 as a Core Number might struggle with relationship stability, job hopping, addictions, commitment, dependence, and independence issues.

Karmic Debt Number 16/7

The 16/7 indicates the misuse of love in a previous life, coupled with a challenge to level one's ego in this lifetime. This Karmic umber pushes individuals to embrace humility and higher purpose through experiences of destruction and rebirth. Those with the 16/7 in their Core Numbers may have been involved in illicit love affairs that caused suffering to others. Traits to grapple with include difficulty in approaching, isolation, struggles in love relationships, aloofness, self-centredness, and emotional detachment.

Before marrying, it is vital to know your karmic number and adjust it. Numerology is a life guide and map. It helps us navigate life's complexities without major setbacks. Embracing these karmic numbers as opportunities for personal growth and evolution is key. Instead of feeling victimised by their influence, use these numbers. They can empower you to clear your karmic slate and move forward with greater insight and wisdom.

Working with a karmic number intensifies the challenges associated with that specific number. It requires your focused commitment, like a test. It tests your ability to change your views on leadership, creativity, ego, achievement, and independence. The familiar, destructive path may seem comfortable. But we must now forge a new, positive way. This transformation not only benefits you but also has positive effects on those around you. In essence, numerology helps us find and fix our karmic challenges. It can lead to better, more fulfilling relationships, especially in marriage.

Chapter 4 : Vedic Astrology

Vedic astrology, or Jyotish, is an ancient Indian astrology. It dates back thousands of years. Celestial bodies, like planets and stars, affect human life and destiny. Vedic astrology originates from the Vedas, India's oldest revered sacred texts. Unlike Western astrology, Vedic astrology stresses karma. It focuses on how past actions affect the present and future.

Vedic astrology is a complex system. It can guide many life aspects, including marriage predictions. It uses a person's birth chart to make predictions. The chart is a map of the positions of celestial bodies at their birth. The birth chart has 12 houses. Each represents a different area of life. It also shows the positions of the planets, their aspects, and conjunctions.

Vedic astrology uses factors to predict marriage. It looks at Venus, the planet of love, and the 7th house in the birth chart, which relates to marriage. Astrologers use these factors, along with the dashas and transits, to predict a person's likely marriage time and method. They assess compatibility by comparing potential partners' birth charts. This determines whether a marriage will be harmonious or face challenges.

In Vedic astrology, Indian tradition holds that marriage is auspicious. The first step is to consult a seasoned Jyotish. They will inspect the wedding horoscope, following the rules of marriage astrology. The first question to an astrologer is always,

"When will I marry?" In response, the skilled Jyotish crafts a deep matrimonial forecast. He studies the complex links between celestial bodies and their Houses.

In astrology, the twelve Sun signs grouped in different ways.

- **Energy/Gender**: Each sign has one of two energies or genders–masculine or feminine.

- **Qualities**: Signs are also divided into three groups called "qualities." Each group has four signs. These groups are Cardinal, Fixed, and Mutable.

- **Elements**: Finally, there are four "elements": Fire, Earth, Air, and Water. Each element contains three signs.

Understanding the Essential Traits of Women from Each Sign and Their Roles in Marriage

Before a deep dive into the complex links of houses, planets, and natal charts, let's first explore the traits of women from each zodiac sign. This talk will explore the traits that define these remarkable people. We explore married life's dynamics. We reveal how women from different zodiac signs navigate relationships and finances as partners.

In Vedic astrology and marriage counselling, it's important to understand the distinct traits and behaviours associated with different zodiac signs when it comes to marriage and finances. Here's how women of different zodiac signs may behave as wives in relation to financial matters:

1. Aries (March 21 - April 19)

Aries wives often want to earn money. They dislike tight budgets. They may encourage their partners to increase their income. They manage finances and save money. But they are intolerant of financial challenges. They dedicate themselves to safeguarding their family's fortune, avoiding frivolous expenditures. It's advisable not to challenge their financial methods.

2. Taurus (April 20 - May 20)

Taurean wives value a comfortable and lavish lifestyle. They prefer a partner with a large income. They value financial security in their relationships. They expect a steady flow of money, without scrimping. If your income is too low, you may need a good excuse for not meeting their financial expectations.

3. Gemini (May 21 - June 20)

Gemini wives may struggle with budgeting. So, it's often the husband's job to handle the finances. They value generous support. It can lead to a happy marriage. But, we must understand their high costs to maintain their appearance.

4. Cancer (June 21 - July 22)

Cancerian wives often delegate financial responsibilities to their partners. They are shrewd in choosing their mates and value family prosperity. They understand the importance of having a home. You may accept financial struggles as long as you commit to your family's welfare.

5. Leo (July 23 - August 22)

Leo wives enjoy a lavish lifestyle. They may struggle to budget for long periods. They look to their partners to make money faster than they can spend it. Leos can motivate their spouses in financial matters. They can also take part-time jobs in a financial emergency.

6. Virgo (August 23 - September 22)

Virgo wives are ambitious and may have their own careers. They have financial freedom and seek intellectual compatibility in relationships. While they may attempt to budget, they may also indulge in spending on personal interests. It's crucial to share both financial and intellectual compatibility with a Virgo wife.

7. Libra (September 23 - October 22)

Libra wives prioritise glamour and luxury and may not handle budgeting well. They avoid arguments about money and expect the best that money can buy. Keep financial worries a secret. Partners should appreciate their charm and looks.

8. Scorpio (October 23 - November 21)

Scorpio wives excel in making the most of a limited income. They are resourceful and creative when it comes to budgeting.

But, they have limits. Husbands should provide enough for a comfortable life without excessive scrimping.

9. Sagittarius (November 22 - December 21)

Sagittarius wives have a desire for adventure and travel. They value independence and pursue moneymaking chances to boost earnings. A partner who can keep up with their dynamic and determined nature is ideal.

10. Capricorn (December 22 - January 19)

Capricorn wives tend to be frugal, avoiding excessive financial restraint. They precision-manage finances and may have skills in trade and barter. Partners should have faith, hope, and courage to complement their responsible nature.

11. Aquarius (January 20 - February 18)

Aquarius wives seek ways to boost their income. They value financial freedom. They have an interest in knowledge and world events. They practice careful management, assessing investment options with precision. Partners should appreciate their independent and intellectual nature.

12. Pisces (February 19 - March 20)

Piscean wives are adaptable and creative with limited resources. They can transform their living spaces with imagination. Partners should support their financial efforts and avoid excessive scrimping.

Astrology offers a broad view of how wives with different zodiac signs may behave with money. Remember, people have different personalities and experiences. Astrological signs are one part of a person's identity.

In Vedic Jyotish (astrology), the 5th house is key in the natal chart. It explores the complex nature of social interactions. This house reveals key aspects of our emotional relationships with others. It shows how we engage in romance. We drawn to or repelled by certain people in love. It also shows the impact these people have on us. Let's explore the implications of the 5th house in Vedic astrology in more detail:

- The 5th house links romance and our emotional expression in those relationships. It explores our approach to love. It looks at the qualities we seek in a partner and how we show affection. It is a house. It reflects our natural inclinations in romance.

- This house shows creativity and the joy of art. It often symbolises a desire to create and procreate, to raise children. The 5th house shows our parenting skills and our bond with our kids.

- Pleasures and enjoyment, including hobbies, are another aspect of the 5th house. This house shows what brings us joy. It reflects our quest for happiness.

- The 5th house sometimes depicts speculation and risk-taking abilities. It covers activities such as gambling and investing. It shows how we handle uncertain ventures and their impact on our lives.

- The 5th house is about romance and friendships. It connects to affectionate bonds. It shows the types of people we bond with and admire in our friends.

- In Vedic astrology, the 7th house is also linked to the 5th house. The 5th house shows whom we attract or repel in love. The 7th house marks the peak of some relationships, like marriage.

The 5th house reveals much about our emotions and social ties. It shows our views on love, creativity, parenting, and fun. In Vedic astrology, the house's placement and planetary influences are key. They shape important aspects of our lives. They offer insights for growth and self-awareness.

This cosmic exploration in astrology focuses on the seventh house, the marriage house. But the astrologer's gaze also covers the second, fifth, and eighth houses. There, they decipher the heavens' cryptic messages. At the heart of this quest are the bright gods, Venus and Jupiter. They are the marriage significators. To assess marriage prospects, check the female's horoscope for Jupiter. Then, check the male's chart for Venus. The celestial guardian Mars, too, holds a pivotal role in this matrimonial soothsaying. Do not overlook the D-9, or Navamsa, chart. Its insights are key to understanding a person's marriage prospects.

A perfect Jyotish studies the marriage horoscope. It reveals a few aspects.:

1. Timing of Matrimony

To solve the marriage riddle, the Jyotish must check three things: the seventh house, its lord, and Venus, the 7th house indicator. They should appear strong and auspicious. An individual's marriage timeline depends on certain marriage yogas. Once found, dictate if the union happens early or late.

The marriage could take place during the 7th house's dasha if everything aligns. In this prophecy, the ascendant lord's dasha and the lord of the 5th house play a significant role. The presence of Venus's dasha can lead to marriage for men. Females often find the hallowed dasha of Jupiter assuming this mantle. The presence of Rahu in the cosmic equation leads to unexpected marriages. The rulers of the 1st, 5th, and 9th houses in the Navamsa chart, along with the associated planets, have influence.

2. Love Marriage or Arranged Marriage

The 5th house represents love in astrology. The 7th House symbolises marriage. The presence of a powerful and unharmed 5th house and its ruling planet indicates the likelihood of a love marriage. The 5th House is filled with celestial beings exuding fiery passion and vibrant energy. The start of a romance is frequently denoted by their mere presence. To determine the likelihood of love or an arranged marriage, pay attention to the

5th and 7th houses, as well as Venus and Mars. The crucial elements for unraveling this cosmic puzzle are the 9th House, representing fortune and its divine ruler.

3. Predictions of the Life Partner

The planets in the seventh house in the astral realm connect the persona of the potential life partner. When Rahu occupies the 7th house of a woman, it suggests a marriage that goes beyond caste or community limitations. When Rahu aligns with the seventh House lord, it signifies a marriage that defies caste boundaries. As for the fairer sex, Jupiter in the 7th house signifies a spouse of sagacious and learned disposition. Thus, the perceptive Jyotish gains valuable understanding about the characteristics of the prospective spouse through the celestial performance in the 7th House.

4. Delay in Matrimony

The reason for the marriage delay might be the adverse impact on the 7th House, it's Lord, and Venus. Jupiter can retrograde, combust, or debilitate. Often, it signifies a marriage put on hold. Mangal Dosha is notorious for causing delays in marriages. Being Saturn and Ketu in the 7th House can delay marriage. When the 7th Lord is in retrograde and Mars occupies the 8th house, it often causes delays in marriage. The feeble presence of the 7th Lord in the 6th or 8th house causes agonizing delays in marriage. A natal chart with both Saturn and Venus, combined with the moon in the 8th or 12th house, suggests a lengthy period before marriage. The Moon's conjunction with Rahu in the 7th House, along with the debilitation of the 7th Lord, increases the chances of a long-lasting marriage.

5. Second Marriage

The arrangement of the stars shows the potential for a second marriage. When multiple planets, Rahu, position themselves in the 7th house, it can cause a series of intricate relationships. If the Lord of the 9th House takes over the 7th House, it could pave the way for a future marriage alliance. When Mars and Venus converge in either the 7th or 9th House, it suggests the chance of marrying again after divorce. Moreover, existing the Lord of the 7th House or the Lord of the 9th House in a dual sign paves the way for a second marriage. The key to fulfilling astrological predictions is a successful alignment of the Dasha and Antardasha periods.

6. Denial of Matrimony

Pravrajya Yoga is a negative sign in Vedic astrology. Being this in the natal chart predicts a denial of marriage. The weak Moon may experience a delay or prevention of marriage because of Saturn's negative influence. If malefic forces surround a feeble 7th house, its sovereign, and Venus, it could cause another impasse. Severe malefic influences on the 9th House can hinder the growth of the marriage yoga in the kundli. In the absence of beneficial influences, this remains accurate.

7. Doshas Impacting Marriage

Troublesome alignments called doshas can disrupt the astrological landscape. They possess the ability to bring unhappiness to marriage. Manglik Dosha, Gana Dosha, Bhakoot Dosha, and Nadi Dosha pose significant challenges in the celestial realm. It is crucial to perform an accurate examination. To assess these doshas, one must be a skilled Jyotish. They must then prescribe remedies to reduce their immense effects.

Also, Vedic astrology has a cosmic tapestry. It shows more vital facets for assessing relationship compatibility.

Ascendant or Lagna: The ascendant sign, also known as Lagna, is the foundation of a birth chart. It acts as a fundamental building block in deciphering one's personality and physical characteristics. When analysing relationships, astrologers focus on the ascendant sign and its celestial bodies. It shows their character and highlights their beautiful features.

Rashi, the Moon sign, represents the intangible world of emotions, feelings, and instincts. Emotional harmony in a relationship depends on a partner's moon sign and its cosmic position. The moon sign reveals how emotions and instincts influence the relationship.

Seventh House: In astrology, the Seventh House symbolises marriage and partnerships. The astrologer analyses the partner's Seventh House, its governing force, and any celestial beings present. By examining this scrutiny, we can gain insight into the partner's stance and approach to relationships and marriage, leading to a better understanding of the dynamics involved.

Eighth House: A careful analysis of the Eighth House is necessary to understand the relationship's endurance and potential hurdles. By exploring the partner's Eighth House and any astral beings present, the astrologer uncovers potential conflicts or challenges that could affect the relationship.

Jupiter: Jupiter, the wise and benevolent guardian, has a significant impact on astrology. To determine intellectual growth and prosperity in the relationship, the perceptive astrologer analyses the partner's Jupiter placement and celestial connections. Jupiter's wisdom and direction act as guiding lights in the path towards unity.

Venus: Venus, the celestial muse of love, romance, and pleasure, weaves a captivating spell over relationships. The astrologer explores the partner's Venus placement and cosmic interactions, revealing the potential for love and romance in the partnership, forming a beautiful tapestry of passion and joy.

Mangal Dosha: The troublesome presence of Mangal Dosha, caused by Mars being positioned in certain houses of a birth chart, can show conflicts and challenges in relationships. The expert astrologer analyzes the partner's chart to identify Mangal Dosha and its consequences for the relationship.

Dashas: Planetary periods, called dashas, determine the rhythm of life events through cosmic currents. The astrologer analyzes the partner's ongoing Dasha period, interpreting how celestial tides influence the relationship. The alignment of planets and their timing plays a crucial role in identifying important shifts and milestones in the partnership.

People across rely on Vedic astrology worldwide when making major life choices, such as marriage. Many people in India and around the world appreciate Vedic astrology for its ability to offer valuable insights into marriage compatibility, timing, and overall success. This helps them make informed decisions about their life partners. This book explores fundamental concepts of the Natal chart, giving readers a basic understanding of personal exploration. To provide readers with essential knowledge for better engagement with astrologers and deeper understanding of their birth charts.

The basic guidelines found with software like "Jagannath Hora" by PVR Narasimha Rao.

By understanding important houses and planets in their birth charts, readers could engage in meaningful conversations with astrologers, ask pertinent questions, and benefit from Vedic astrology's wisdom and guidance. This foundational knowledge guide your journey of self-discovery and personal growth through the lens of a Vedic horoscope.

Official Website: https://www.vedicastrologer.org/jh/

Please note that software availability and websites may change occasionally, so I recommend doing an internet search or visiting the official website to confirm the most up-to-date information on how to download the software.

In the quest for genuine astrological compatibility, one must not disregard these integral facets. It's time to unveil the celestial charts and delve into the profound prerequisites for evaluating matrimonial suitability, whether you are considering an arranged alliance or a love union.

Celestial Star Harmony

It's important to compare your celestial stars (nakshatras) with your partner's before embarking on your marital journey. The solar manifestations of both you and your partner expose their inherent alignment through this metric. The kundali contains 27 nakshatras. There is an abundance of digital instruments for evaluating celestial calibration. Remember, nakshatra harmony is just a small part, accounting for only 35% of the total matching equation. It provides a thorough insight into the alignment of your fates and alerts you to possible obstacles in your relationship.

Synchronicity of Soul and Venus Signs

If Sun and Venus signs align in the same zodiac constellation, it unveils a tapestry of insights into your partner's past relationships. Through this alignment, we get a glimpse into their previous partners and the characteristics that captivated them. Evaluate the possibility of marital compatibility by understanding their perspective and aligning it with your own. Your marriage has the capability to be a significant milestone in your life journey.

Venus's Astral Position in a Kundli

Symbolising affection and warmth, Venus is a crucial figure in astrology. The birth chart of your partner tells a cosmic narrative of their intense emotional expression. The perfect alignment of Venus in your astrological charts guarantees a joyful marriage with excellent communication and everlasting affection. It is crucial to acknowledge that a negative setup has the potential to hinder expressing affection and reduce marital happiness.

Venus holds significance in astrology due to its association with affection, romance, and connections. It has a significant impact on various areas of life, including personal connections, values, aesthetics, and social interactions. Let's explore the crucial domains where Venus holds reasonable sway:

1. Love and Relationships: For love and romantic relationships, Venus takes the lead. By examining its position in a person's birth chart, we can learn about their love style, preferred partners, and ability to create long-lasting relationships.

2. Aesthetics: Good looks, and individual style are under Venus's jurisdiction. It influences an individual's sense of fashion, artistic preferences, and appreciation of art, music, and pleasing things.

3. Values and Finances: Venus governs personal values, including what an individual considers important or valuable

in life. One can extend this to their financial attitudes, spending habits, and material possessions.

4. Social Skills and Charm: People with strong Venus placements often have charisma, grace, and social finesse. With their increased charisma and adeptness at building positive relationships, they can excel in various social and professional contexts.

5. Creativity and Artistic Expression: Venus inspires artistic expression and creativity. Showing an individual's artistic talents and potential for innovative pursuits, its placement in a birth chart may involve painting, music, writing, or other forms of self-style.

6. Venus connects to marriage and long-term partnerships. By revealing the qualities an individual seeks in a life partner and the nature of their marital relationships, its placement can offer insights.

7. Emotional Well-Being: A harmonious Venus can contribute to emotional well-being and a positive outlook on love and relationships. Challenging aspects of Venus may show difficulties in forming and maintaining sentimental connections.

8. Self-Worth and Self-Esteem: Venus influences an individual's self-worth and self-esteem, as they are associated with their ability to attract and support love and affection. A powerful Venus has the potential to enhance self-confidence,

while a difficult Venus placement may cause self-doubt and insecurity.

9. Sensuality and Pleasure: Venus governs sensuality, pleasure, and enjoyment in life. Each individual can showcase their approach to sensual experiences.

The influence of Venus in astrology goes beyond matters of love and romance, making it a multifaceted planet. It is essential for shaping an individual's values, aesthetics, social interactions, and overall sense of well-being. By having the ability to comprehend their Venus position, people can understand different areas of their lives and apply this information to navigate their personal connections and life decisions more efficiently.

If your birth had Venus in Aries, you have confidence and a lively imagination. You have the power to heighten the sincerity in others to incredible levels. Your inconsistency and unpredictable behaviour could create disharmony in your romantic affairs. Infusing stability, reliability, and kindness into your beliefs can foster deep and long-lasting bonds.

When Venus is in Taurus, you show patience, possessiveness, and caution in relationships. Your overwhelming need for safety may make you hesitant to embrace love, but once you do, your love becomes steadfast. Your possessiveness may make your partner feel trapped. Enhancing trust and minimising possessiveness can have a positive impact on your love life.

With Venus in Gemini, your feelings are more intellectual than emotional. You rank the intellectual elements of love and romance, often valuing mental stimulation more than physical affection. Exploring mental compatibility can ease restlessness and potential relationship conflicts.

Welcoming Venus into Cancer means you have a receptive, and affectionate nature. Your deep affection for your home and family is remarkable. Discovering a middle ground and maintaining moderation can foster greater harmony in your relationships.

Your loyalty, reliability, and geniality are your strengths if Venus was in Leo at your birth. Although you have a magnetic and social personality, your need for attention and personal pride can overshadow your relationships. Spreading kindness, humility, and putting others first can cause deeper love.

When Venus is in Virgo, you approach love with analysis and discrimination. Emotional suppression or emphasis on personal ethics and morality may result from this. Pursuing understanding, tolerance, and kindness leads to a gentler, more gratifying love.

With Venus in Libra, you enjoy a refined and idealistic nature. You value harmony and want a pleasant environment in your relationships. The extremes of your refinement and aversion to vulgarity can cause you to experience periods of aloofness. Balancing kindness and tolerance can lead to the harmony you are exploring.

Having Venus in Scorpio means intensity and passion, which characterises your love nature. Your emotions have the potential to swing from intense highs to extreme lows, resulting in either profound or diminished experiences. Instead of extreme actions, practicing self-discipline can lead to a more fulfilling and passionate love that benefits both you and your loved ones.

Placing Venus in Sagittarius shows a love for nature that is driven by aspirations and a need for constant change. Sometimes, your wish for new experiences can misguide you. Achieving emotional stability and happiness involves balancing personal desires and others' expectations.

People approach love in a conservative and practical manner when Venus is in Capricorn. Personal romance may not be as important to you compared to ethics and material success. Discovering kindness, tolerance, and flexibility can lead to harmonious relationships.

Your Venus in Aquarius acknowledges a deep sense of contemplation and introspection in matters of love. Balancing your want for personal freedom with consideration for others can lead to more stable and harmonious relationships.

When Venus is in Pisces, you gain an affectionate, intuitive, and idealistic nature. When Venus is in Pisces, you notice a clear and compassionate love, but it may not always be a priority. Your ability to understand and aid those in need can bring depth and meaning to your relationships.

The Governing Luminary of the Ascendant House

We have studied the celestial bodies that govern the domains where the couple is getting ready for their wedding. The Lagna house, also known as the ascendant house, plays a central role in this interplay. A harmonious union is impossible without the ascendant's compatibility or Lagna, as per Vedic astrological doctrine. When these components oppose each other, strenuous trials may mark marriage, contrasting perspectives, and ongoing discord.

Mercury's Astral Placement in Kundli

Mercury is the ruler of communication in Kundli's tapestry. Therefore, discerning Mercury's placement in your partner's natal chart is pivotal. The fortuitous alignment suggests wisdom and skill in expressing profound thoughts. This fosters meaningful conversations and easy problem-solving within the marriage.

The Kundali's Seventh House

The seventh house in your partner's astrological chart is significant, representing the core of marriage in astrology. It reveals the core of a partnership, including attitudes and the atmosphere of one's married life. Exploring the zodiac sign and celestial beings within it can reveal valuable insights into your compatibility with your partner. The presence of celestial bodies, including the moon, in this house provides valuable information about your future life partner. Their personalities might display a dominant, self-reliant, and influential nature, combined with charm and empathy.

In astrology, the 7th house is associated with marriage and partnerships. Placing planets in the 7th house can impact marriage and relationships. Below, I summarise how the planets in the 7th house influences marriage and partnerships, focusing on Rahu (Uranus) and Ketu (Neptune).

SUN (Surya): Marriage becomes a vivid and joyous experience when the sun is in the 7th house. For marriage, people place emphasis on honesty, loyalty, and ethical values. Caution is necessary when dealing with the sun's desire for authority and power to prevent relationship conflicts.

MOON (Chandra): The Moon's placement in the 7th house brings a touch of romance to love and marriage, but it may bring about mood swings and emotional conflicts. Sometimes, the focus on household and family duties can overshadow the romance in a marriage. Many people share the goal of creating a happy home.

MERCURY (Budha): Being Mercury in the 7th house affects your temperament and can lead to various intellectual and emotional changes in your marriage. For a fortunate marriage, it's crucial to have meaningful conversations, shared interests, and intellectual stimulation. The helpful marriage can be attributed to the adaptability and exceptional communication skills of this placement.

VENUS (Shukra): When Venus is in the 7th house, it brings many benefits to love and marriage. Venus embodies love, affection, and pleasure, making it a symbol of harmonious relationships. This positioning results in a joyful and pleasing marriage, placing importance on gentleness, artistic inclinations, and a tranquil setting.

MARS (Mangal): Marital relationships may experience heightened passion and aggression when Mars is in the 7th house. Signifying physical love and the common desire for emotional intensity. Yet, this can cause conflicts and impatience as well. To have a successful marriage with Mars in the 7th house, balance passion and patience.

JUPITER (Guru): If Jupiter is in the 7th house, it's a sign of favourable outcomes in matters of love and marriage. Relationships with this placement require loyalty, devotion, and harmony. Typical traits include a firm commitment and a desire for a well-rounded marriage.

SATURN (Shani): Being Saturn in the 7th house can lead to difficulties and delays when deciding on marriage. Although it brings responsibilities and a sense of duty, it can also result in harsh judgments and a tendency to be realistic, often ignoring dreams and fantasies. A happy marriage requires balancing patience, reliability, and understanding.

RAHU (Uranus): Marriage takes on an exciting and unpredictable nature when Uranus is in the 7th house. Nothing is more important than independence and the longing for freedom. Partners in marriage should allow for individual freedom and be receptive to unconventional and progressive perspectives.

KETU (Neptune): The presence of Neptune in the 7th house adds a mystical and idealistic touch to love and marriage. Relationships lose their appeal when focused on material aspects, while spiritual and idealistic elements remain essential. Yet, when Neptune is aspected, it can create confusion and disorder in marriage, highlighting the need for clarity and stability.

One's marriage and partnerships are greatly affected by the planets in the 7th house. Each planet contributes distinct qualities and difficulties in relationships, and recognising these impacts can assist individuals in navigating their marriages better.

Mars's Celestial Position in Kundli

Mars, the celestial embodiment of desire and passion, rules over the celestial sphere. Analyzing its placement in your partner's birth chart allows you to measure the compatibility of your emotional and physical desires. Understanding your partner's desires in both the physical and emotional aspects of your relationship becomes easier.

Mars influences the emotional dynamics within the marriage. Learning about Mars's position helps you navigate and fulfil your partner's aspirations in the matrimonial bond.

The potential of astrology lies in its ability to offer profound insights into the dynamics of your connection and your partner's inherent character. Considering various aspects like charm, connection, emotional balance, family dynamics, passion, money matters, commitment, and sexual compatibility can aid in making an informed choice about marriage. However, it's crucial to acknowledge that astrology is only a small part of the puzzle. A successful marriage requires a combination of understanding, respect, and effective communication.

In Vedic astrology, determining marriage compatibility involves both the guna milan (ashtakoot guna matching), analysis of planets and houses in the individual's natal charts, including the D1 and D9 charts. Here's how these aspects are considered:

Guna Milan (Ashtakoot Guna Matching) : This is the initial step in assessing marriage compatibility. Guna milan involves the matching of eight key factors (kootas) in the horoscopes of both individuals:

- Varna (1 point): Assessing the spiritual development and compatibility of the couple.

In Vedic astrology, the concept of Varna or Jati refers to a classification system used to categorise individuals based on their ego or self-identity, which in turn associated with specific qualities, roles, and responsibilities. There are four main Varnas or Jatis in this system:

1. Brahmana: This Varna represents individuals with qualities associated with knowledge, learning, and spirituality. People in

this category traditionally include scholars, priests, teachers, and spiritual leaders. They are expected to focus on learning, intellectual pursuits, and spiritual growth. Cancer, Scorpio and Pisces are the examples.

2. Kshatriya: The kshatriya varna is associated with qualities related to strength, courage, leadership, and protection. Those in this category often seen as warriors, rulers, and defenders of society. They take on roles involves governance, defence, and the protection of others. Aries, Leo and Sagittarius.

3. Vaishya: Individuals in the vaishya varna are associated with qualities related to commerce, trade, and economic activities. They traditionally include businesspeople, traders, farmers, and merchants. Their primary roles involve commerce, trade, and wealth generation. Taurus, Virgo and Capricorn.

4. Shudra: The shudra varna is associated with qualities such as service, labor, and support. Those in this category often serve other varnas and are traditionally considered as labourers, artisans, and service providers. Their primary roles involve supporting other varnas in their respective tasks. Gemini, Libra and Aquarius.

Couples belongs to the same varna gets 1(one) Guna. The woman belonging to a higher varna than the man is inauspicious. The reason is the lack of temperamental compatibility. Similar professional background is good for relationships. Understanding each other's professions and the stresses helps to maintain a balanced lifestyle.

In traditional Vedic astrology, believers hold the belief that for a marriage to be harmonious and compatible, the Varnas of the bride and groom should match or have a specific compatibility pattern. The general rule for compatibility is that the groom's varna should be at least one point higher than that of the bride. This means that the groom should belong to a varna with higher qualities and responsibilities than that of the bride.

If varna matching is not carried out, people perceive it as incompatible, and such a union may encounter challenges or disharmony. This aspect is one of several factors considered in Vedic astrology in determining a prospective marriage.

It's important to note that while Vedic astrology provides these traditional guidelines, contemporary practices and beliefs about compatibility in marriages can vary, and many individuals do not place significant emphasis on the Varna or Jati factor when choosing a life partner. Modern couples often prioritize factors like shared values, interests, and emotional compatibility over the traditional Vedic astrology classifications.

- Vashya (2 points): Evaluating the mutual control and dominance between the partners. It also mens attraction, its important in understanding the mutual attraction. This attraction will indicate their ability to influence each other.

Vashya, in the context of Vedic astrology, is a classification system used to assess the power dynamic or compatibility between the bride and the groom. It categorises humans into five groups, and each associated with specific qualities and characteristics. These groups are as follows:

1. Manav Vashya (Human): This category includes individuals who are seen as rational, empathetic, and capable of forming emotional connections. Human vashya indicates compatibility based on shared human traits. Gemini, Virgo, Libra and first half of Sagittarius.

2. Banachara Vashya (Wild Animals): Those classified under this category are associated with qualities of independence and self-reliance, much like wild animals. It signifies a power dynamic based on individuality and self-sufficiency.

3. Chatushpad Vashya (Small Animals): Individuals belonging to this category appears gentle, adaptable, and cooperative. Suggests compatibility through mutual cooperation and adaptability. Aries, Taurus, latter half of Sagittarius and first half of Capricorn.

4. Jalachara Vashya (Waterborne Animals): This vashya is associated with qualities of fluidity, emotional depth, and adaptability. Waterborne animals often signify the need for emotional connection and depth in the power dynamic. Cancer, second half of Capricorn, Aquarius and Pisces.

5. Keeta or insect Vashya (Insects): The Keet represents individuals with qualities of restlessness, constant activity, and change. Suggests a power dynamic characterised by constant movement and change. Scorpio.

To assess compatibility using the Vashya system, a scoring system is employed:

- When the bride and the groom belong to the same Vashya, they receive a compatibility score of 2 points.

- If they belong to opposite, the compatibility score is zero, indicating potential challenges in the power dynamic.

- When there is a combination of Manav (Human) and Jalchar (Waterborne Animals), they receive 1/2 point as a compatibility score.

- For all other combinations not mentioned above, a compatibility score of 1 point is given.

This Vashya system is just one of several factors considered in Vedic astrology for assessing the compatibility of a potential marriage. While it provides traditional guidelines, it's important to note that modern couples often prioritize other aspects, such as shared values, interests, and emotional compatibility, over the traditional astrological classifications when making decisions about their relationships and marriages.

Tara (3 points): Examining the health and well-being of the couple. Count the Nakshatra from the female to the nakshatra of the male (Moon nakshatra). Do the same from the male to female. In case the distance is bigger that 9 - divide it by nine.

Birth star compatibility, also known as "Nakshatra compatibility," is a significant factor in Vedic astrology when assessing the compatibility of a potential marriage. In this

ANIMAL	NAKSHATRA	MALE	FEMALE
Horse	Ashwini & Satabisha	Ashwini	Satabisha
Elephant	Bharani & Revati	Bharani	Revati
Sheep	Kritika & Pushya	Kritika	Pushya
Serpent	Rohini & Mrigarshira	Rohini	Mrigashira
Dog	Ardra & Moola	Ardra	Moola
Cat	Punarvasu & Ashlesha	Punarvasu	Ashlesha
Rat	Magha & Purva Phalguni	Magha	Purva Phalguni
Cow	Uttar Phalguni & Uttar Bhadrapada	Uttar Phalguni	Uttar Bhadrapada
Buffalo	Hasta & Swati	Hasta	Swati
Tiger	Chitra & Vishaka	Chitra	Vishaka
Deer	Anuradha & Jyestha	Anuradha	Jyestha
Monkey	Purva Ashada & Sravana	Purva Ashada	Sravana
Mongoose	Uttar Ashada	Uttar Ashada	No Animal*
Lion	Dhanistha & Purva Bhadrapada	Dhanistha	Purva Bhadrapada

system, each individual is associated with one of the 27 Nakshatras, which are lunar constellations or star signs.

The compatibility score is determined by a specific calculation involving the Nakshatras of both the bride and the groom:

1. The Nakshatra of the bride is counted from that of the groom. The number obtained is then divided by nine.

2. Similarly, the Nakshatra of the groom is counted from that of the bride, and the resultant number is divided by nine.

3. The remainder, or the leftover value after division by nine, is then examined for both the bride and the groom.

The compatibility score is determined based on the nature of these remainders:

- If both the bride's and the groom's remainders are even, the compatibility score is 3. This indicates a high level of compatibility.

- If both the remainders are odd, the compatibility score is zero. This suggests a lack of compatibility.

- If one of the remainders is even, and the other is odd, the compatibility score is 1.5 points. This signifies a moderate level of compatibility.

The compatibility assessment, along with other astrological factors, offers insights into the harmony or challenges in a marriage. Modern couples take multiple factors into account, such as shared values and emotional compatibility, when deciding on their relationships and marriages, despite it being a traditional aspect of Vedic astrology.

Yoni (4 points): The sexual compatibility and harmony between the partners. Yoni means female sexual organ. The nakshatras are divided into female and male animal energies.

Ideal sexual compatibility between the male and female of the same animal species like Pushya and Krittika - the masculine and feminine of the Sheep.

In Vedic astrology, Yoni Koot, or sexual compatibility, is one of the aspects considered when assessing the compatibility between a bride and groom. Associated with the classification of individuals into 14 categories, each represented by an animal. These categories used to determine the level of sexual compatibility between the couple. Throughout the ages, we've evolved from our primal animal ancestors. No matter how sophisticated and modern we consider ourselves, a powerful animal instinct still resides within us.

In Vedic Astrology, each person is associated with an animal symbol, reflecting the inherent attributes of that creature in their personality.

Have you ever pondered your ancestral lineage? If not, Vedic Astrology provides insight into pedigree. Janam Nakshatra or birth star, unveils the kind of breed that resides within.

This science recognises 27 Janam Nakshatras or birth stars. Each individual typically has up to nine Nakshatras in their birth chart, corresponding to nine grahas or planets. We refer to 'Janam Nakshatra,' associated with the Moon.

The Moon, akin to the Sun, holds a special place in Vedic Astrology, representing the mind. Our choices, whether it's the music or the food often driven by the mind's preferences.

As the mind guides the action, the specific Nakshatra where the Moon is placed or gazing upon reveals much about our individual attributes. Thus, the Janam Nakshatra provides valuable insights into a person's characteristics and general interests, even without delving into their birth chart.

If two male nakshatras marry it may led to incompatibility and the same with the two female. The compatibility score is calculated based on the classification of the animals of the bride and groom. Here is how the scoring system works:

- If the bride and groom belong to the same animal category, they receive a perfect score of 4 points. This suggests a high level of sexual compatibility.

- The animals are considered enemies in the classification (for example, a cat and a dog), the compatibility score is zero points. This indicates potential challenges in the realm of sexual compatibility.

- When the animals are considered friendly in the classification (for example, a horse and an elephant), the compatibility score is 3 points, signifying a good level of compatibility.

- The animals are neutral to each other (for example, a sheep and a buffalo), the compatibility score is 2 points.

- When the animals appears non-friendly but not enemies (for example, a snake and a rat), the compatibility score is 1 point.

Rashish (5 points): Analyzing the intellectual and emotional compatibility.

Gana (6 points): Evaluating the temperament and nature of the individuals.

Rashi (7 points): Assessing financial prosperity and family welfare.

Nadi (8 points): Checking for genetic compatibility and the presence of genetic disorders.

Each of these gunas has a specific set of rules for assessing compatibility. The total score helps astrologers determine whether the prospective couple is a good match. However, it's important to note that while Vedic astrology provides a framework for evaluating compatibility, individual compatibility involves many other factors, including personal values, lifestyle, and communication. People should use astrology as a guideline but not the sole determining factor for choosing a life partner.

Planets and Houses in D1 Chart (Natal Chart): In addition to guna milan, Vedic astrologers analyze the placement and aspects of planets in the individual's natal (D1) chart. The 5th and 7th houses play a crucial role in predicting marriage.

5th House: The 5th house is associated with romance, love affairs, and progeny. The planets placed in the 5th house, as well as the signs and aspects to this house, can provide insights into the romantic inclinations of an individual. This house can indicate the potential for romantic relationships and the type of partner one attracts.

7th House: The 7th house is the primary house of marriage and partnerships. The planets in the 7th house, their aspects, and the sign on the cusp of the 7th house provide information about the individual's marriage and the characteristics of their spouse.

D9 Chart (Navamsa Chart): The D9 chart, also known as the Navamsa chart, is a divisional chart that provides insights into the finer and deeper aspects of an individual's life, including marriage. Astrologers often consider the following factors in the D9 chart:

Planetary Placements: The placement of planets in the Navamsa chart can reveal important information about the soul's purpose and the quality of the marital relationship.

Navamsa Lagna (Ascendant): The Navamsa Lagna and its ruler are key indicators of the overall quality of marriage and the individual's spouse.

Aspects and Combustion: The aspects between planets in the Navamsa chart and any combustion (planets too close to the Sun) are important considerations.

By analysing the D9 chart in conjunction with the D1 chart, astrologers can gain a deeper understanding of the potential dynamics and outcomes of a marriage.

Here are the basic guidelines to follow when creating your D1 and D9 charts using astrology software, which can provide you with a foundational understanding. However, for a comprehensive analysis and professional guidance, it is advisable to consult an experienced Vedic astrologer who offers deeper insights and interpretations based on these charts.

1. Absence of Malefic Planet Aspects in the Seventh House

It is imperative that the Seventh House, representing marriage, remains free from the malefic influences of planets. Malefic planets are considered antagonistic to this house. For instance, if Rahu, Saturn, Mars, Sun, or Ketu cast negative aspects on the Seventh House, it can lead to complications in both love and marital life.

2. Nadi Dosha

Nadi Dosha plays a pivotal role in assessing relationship compatibility through Vedic Astrology. The presence of Nadi Dosha in a natal chart can result in challenges related to future offspring, including delays in conception, miscarriages, and abortions. A thorough analysis of the natal charts of both partners can help anticipate and address such issues in advance.

3. Malefic Planet Conjunction in the Seventh House

Difficulties may arise in a relationship or marriage if either partner associated malefic planets in the Seventh House. Such complications may escalate into more significant problems like separation, engaging in multiple relationships, instability in relationships, and emotional upheaval. Some problematic planetary conjunctions in the Seventh House include Mars with Saturn, Venus with the Sun, and Rahu with Mars. Vedic Astrology analyses various combinations in a person's natal chart.

4. Placement of the Lord of the Seventh House

The placement of the Lord of the Seventh House, which governs marriage, plays a significant role in the natal charts of both partners. Lord of the Seventh House should not be located in unfavourable positions or form adverse aspects, especially involving planets like Rahu and Ketu. These combinations commonly known as 'Grahan Yogas.'

5. Degrees of the Lord of the Seventh House

The balance of degrees in the Lord of the Seventh House (House of Marriage) is crucial. An imbalance, either with excessively high or low degrees impacts the love or married life.

Astrologers consider other factors like astrological compatibility, planetary aspects, influences from other houses and moon signs, as well as the ascendant's effects on each individual, to evaluate relationship compatibility.

According to Vedic Astrology, these five major points are crucial for assessing partner compatibility in relationships. Not paying attention to them can hinder reaching a definite conclusion. Thus, for a more precise outcome, it is crucial to evaluate these five essential factors when seeking a compatibility assessment.

While astrology provides valuable insights, it's important to remember that marriage is a complex and multifaceted institution. Personal choices, communication, mutual respect, and emotional compatibility all play a role in the compatibility and success of a marriage. Astrology used as a self-awareness and guidance, not as an absolute predictor of marital fate.

Marriage and partnerships are influenced by the 7th house in Vedic astrology. Existing different planets in the 7th house can affect your relationships and marital life in distinct ways. Let's break down these planetary placements into simpler terms:

Rahu in all houses

Rahu in 1st House: Individuals with Rahu in the 1st house are self-centred and materialistic. Their desire for fame and popularity may lead to concerns about their public image. Their enigmatic charm influence and manipulate others. Some of these individuals might find it hard to achieve satisfaction and may engage in risky behaviors in order to fill an emotional void.

Rahu in 2nd House: When Rahu is in the 2nd house, it can create a strong longing for material success and wealth, often through unconventional methods. It's common for people to overspend and accumulate debt. Rahu's positioning impact the 6th, 8th, and 10th houses, fostering industriousness, a craving for authority, and an aspiration for fame in one's career.

Rahu in 3rd House: The 3rd house represents communication and siblings. Rahu here makes individuals ambitious, competitive, and skilled communicator. They are gifted for persuasive speaking and learning languages. Power and recognition remains vital as goals.

Rahu in 4th House: Existing Rahu in the 4th house may lead to restlessness and discontentment concerning home, family, and emotional stability. Family dynamics can be nontraditional, and it's possible to have a difficult relationship with one's mother. Rahu's aspects influence the 8th, 10th, and 12th houses, which affect financial and emotional stability.

Rahu in 5th House: When Rahu is in the 5th house, there is a strong inclination for material pleasures that can cause risky actions. The individual struggles to find fulfilment due to hindered pursuit of creativity. Spirituality and philosophy may become intriguing because of Rahu's impact on the 9th house.

Rahu in 6th House: Rahu in the 6th house often makes individuals ambitious and competitive. They possess the drive to succeed and overcome challenges. However, an excessive obsession with their goals may lead to self-sabotage. They aim for prominent positions of authority in their chosen field.

Rahu in 7th House: Rahu in the 7th house significantly impacts personal and professional relationships. This placement is generally considered unfavourable. Individuals drawn to unconventional partners and struggle to find stability and commitment in relationships. Restlessness and dissatisfaction lead to a tendency to seek new partners or business opportunities.

If Rahu is in the 7th house of a birth chart, it greatly impacts one's relationships and marriage. According to Vedic astrology, the 7th house represents partnerships, marriage, and committed relationships. Let me provide you with a comprehensive understanding of the impact of Rahu in the 7th house:

Unconventional relationships: When Rahu is in the 7th house, it often leads to a strong longing for unconventional relationships. People with this position often gravitate towards partners who challenge societal norms or have unconventional backgrounds. They look for excitement, variety, and novelty in their relationships, choosing experiences that differ from the usual. This tendency result in relationships that deviate from the norm, catching others off guard.

Intensity and Passion: Rahu's presence in the 7th house intensifies the individual's longing for passionate and intense connections. There exists a powerful desire for emotional and physical experiences within their relationships. This heightened intensity results in dramatic emotional highs and lows, creating a rollercoaster-like dynamic in their partnerships. The intensity makes their relationships captivating but challenging.

Challenging Relationships: Challenges and complexities in relationships can arise because of Rahu's influence in the 7th house. People in relationships may face unforeseen situations, sudden shifts, or feel uncertainty. Difficulties arise from the unpredictable nature, hindering stability and harmonious relationships. Striving for equilibrium is a perpetual challenge.

Unresolved Karmic Issues: Those with Rahu in the 7th house have karmic lessons to learn in relationships. Trust, power dynamics, compromise, and balancing personal desires with partner needs are common themes in these lessons. These people are working through past-life problems by navigating their relationships.

Attraction to Unavailable Partners: When Rahu is in the 7th house, it can cause a desire for unavailable partners or create relationship complications. The 7th house placement of Rahu can complicate relationships and cause individuals to be attracted to those who are unavailable or incompatible. Complex emotional entanglements and turmoil can arise from longing for the unattainable.

Focus on Material Gain: Those with Rahu in the 7th house may prioritise material gain and financial aspects in their relationships. They may look for partners who can offer financial stability and boost their social standing. Finding a balance between material wealth and emotional/spiritual aspects is crucial in relationships.

The influence of Rahu in the 7th house can differ depending on other planetary placements, aspects, and personal circumstances. By consulting a seasoned Vedic astrologer, individuals can gain a more nuanced and personalised insight into the specific effects of Rahu in the 7th house on their life and relationships. An astrologer could provide remedies and guidance to navigate challenges and leverage opportunities in this birth chart placement.

Rahu in 8th House: Placing Rahu in the 8th house is considered unfavourable. It may cause restlessness, anxiety, and a fascination with unconventional or taboo topics. It's tough to overcome addictions and compulsive behaviours. The 12th house's aspect of Rahu can impact both financial and emotional stability.

Rahu in 9th House: The 9th house's Rahu affects spirituality, higher education, and travel. It might create knowledge and spirituality. It could make people seem smart, but without true beliefs. Curiosity drives a desire to roam and explore. It seeks to learn about diverse beliefs, customs, and ways of life. This quest for knowledge drives adventurers to cross borders. They seek to unravel the tapestry of human experience. With open minds and restless spirits, they seek wisdom in the unknown. They embrace the richness of our global mosaic of philosophies.

Rahu in the 10th House: Rahu is in the 10th house of a birth chart, it brings a mix of good and bad effects on one's career and public image. People know Rahu for its ambition and materialism. It creates a strong desire to gain success and recognition in one's field.

On the positive side, Rahu in the 10th house can bring fame. It is especially true in high-profile fields like politics, media, and entertainment.

Rahu in the 11th House: Rahu's most auspicious position is in the 11th house. This house refers gains, earnings, and fulfilling desires. People see this placement as a sign of future success, wealth, and fame. Those with Rahu in the 11th house have a vast, influential social circle. Their strong networking skills help them achieve their goals.

Rahu's condition of the 3rd house boosts communication and negotiation skills. These are key to maintaining good relationships with siblings, colleagues, and business partners. They make local trips that boost their income.

Rahu in the 12th House: The presence of Rahu in the 12th house presents distinct challenges, symbolising loss and excessive spending. It sparks a desire for luxurious living, which can lead to financial worries. The placement of Rahu in the 12th house can bring about opportunities for success in foreign lands and global exploration.

When Rahu influences the 4th house, it creates complications involving one's home and their relationship with their mother. Placing someone here could cause a lack of emotional support from the mother and make them make them feel detachment from their home country. Health problems, especially those stemming from hidden ailments, may arise because of Rahu's influence on the 6th house. it appears as new enemies and challenges in everyday situations.

Planets aspect the 5th, 7th, and 9th houses from their position. if the Sun is in Aries, it aspects the 5th (Leo), 7th (Libra), and 9th (Sagittarius) houses.

- **Jupiter**: Jupiter aspects the 5th and 9th houses, promoting growth and wisdom.

o **Mars**: Mars also aspects the 4th and 8th houses, adding intensity to home life, emotions, and transformation.

o **Saturn**: Besides the 7th house, Saturn aspects the 3rd and 10th houses, emphasizing discipline in communication and career.

These special aspects are particularly influential, shaping key areas of an individual's life

Planetary Aspects on the 7th House

The realm of astrology has been a longstanding guide for understanding the intricate dynamics of relationships and marriage. It teaches us that the positions of planets in various houses can exert a profound influence on different aspects of our lives, with marriage being no exception. In this exploration, we will delve into the impact of planetary aspects on the 7th house, which has a traditional association with partnerships, commitments, and marital bonds.

Saturn's Influence on 7th House Marriages

Saturn, the zodiac's taskmaster, brings responsibility and order to our relationships. When it casts its influence on the 7th house, it leads to delays in marriage. Partnerships often exhibit strength and endurance because of delays. Saturn's influence may challenge couples. But these trials can help their relationship grow.

Rahu's Aspects and Effect on 7th House Marriages

Rahu in the 7th house can cause intense, unconventional partnerships. This could lead to sudden, unexpected marriages with diverse partners. It's vital to approach such relationships with caution. They may bring uncertainties and challenges.

Jupiter's Positive Impact on 7th House Marriages

A sense of positivity and happiness surrounds the union when Jupiter blesses the 7th house. Its influence infuses partnerships with luck, expansion, and a sense of harmony. Jupiter may bring a supportive, caring spouse and togetherness.

Mercury's Role in 7th House Relationships

When Mercury graces the 7th house, communication rules the relationship. Partners may share intellectual compatibility and engaging in meaningful conversations. Yet, this can cause overthinking and lengthy discussions. It may lead to misunderstandings that need careful handling.

Venus and Its Influence on the 7th House

Venus, the planet of love and beauty, rules the 7th house. It boosts the romantic and artistic sides of partnerships. This aspect signifies love, affection, and sensuality in relationships. Couples touched by Venus may feel a deep bond. They will enjoy shared pleasures and experiences.

Mars Energising the 7th House

Mars's aspect in the 7th house infuses relationships with passion, drive, and energy. This can lead to exciting and adventurous partnerships. However, we must manage any conflicts or power struggles that may arise. Mars's influence makes open communication and compromise vital for a healthy relationship.

The Sun's Radiance in 7th House Relationships

The Sun in the 7th house brings vitality to partnerships. It signifies a strong identity within the relationship. Couples may find themselves supporting each other's ambitions and encouraging personal growth. However, the Sun's influence can also give rise to ego clashes if not managed with care.

The Moon's Influence on Emotional Connections

When the nurturing Moon aspects the 7th house, emotions rule relationships. Connection and empathy are key. Partners may share a profound emotional bond and focus on each other's feelings. But, this can cause mood swings that need patience and understanding.

Ketu's Spiritual Dimension in 7th House

Ketu's aspect on the 7th house adds a spiritual, karmic element to partnerships. This aspect may lead to unconventional or non-traditional unions. It offers a unique view on relationships. But, we must address any detachment. We should work to stay connected.

It's important to keep in mind, as we wrap up the chapter on astrology compatibility, that understanding astrological signs is just a small part of building a thriving relationship. Going beyond mere compatibility, working on and preparing for the relationship you want is crucial. Two people often desire to be together, but misunderstandings can arise regarding the true nature of that desire. We can align our desires and intentions by clarifying the language we use to talk about relationships. A visual relationship map can provide a new outlook on how past connections influence your present.

Many people desire a partner, but often neglect to define the true meaning of a relationship, assuming mutual understanding. Asking yourself: What are my relationship desires? is crucial. Who do I imagine being in it alongside me? What is its purpose? Is it for friendship, companionship, intimacy, or maybe something more specific like marriage or financial support? Record your responses, evaluate them, and contemplate if they align with your wishes. Whether you're in a current relationship or thinking about a past one, this exercise can be eye-opening.

Begin documenting your thoughts, insights, and reactions in a journal as you delve into these questions. This exercise aids in uncovering your authentic desires and navigating complex relationships with enhanced clarity and intent.

Chapter 5 : Astro-numerology

In the last chapter, we explored Vedic Astrology. It uses celestial influences to guide personal and spiritual growth. This is ancient Indian wisdom. We studied planetary positions and aspects. They shape our destinies. Vedic Astrology is ancient. It helps us understand cosmic influences on our lives. It does this through detailed planetary charts and astrological houses.

Now, we shift our focus. We will move from the Vedic view to a blend of astrology and numerology. This added dimension, called Astro Numerology, merges the two fields. It offers a better understanding of our personalities and life paths. Astro Numerology blends the energies of numbers with astrological symbols. It shows how cosmic and numerical influences intersect and interact in our lives.

In this chapter, we will delve into the connection between astrology and numerology. You'll gain proficiency in applying these principles. Your understanding of personal traits will be enhanced by them. They are useful for anticipating upcoming trends.

Astro-Numerology makes it easier to overcome life's challenges. It would assist you in capitalising on opportunities with a more focused sense of guidance.

Astro Numerology reveals the mysteries of your life by connecting the stars and numbers.

Astro Numerology is a metaphysical field. It combines astrology and numerology. It helps to understand personality, life events, and cosmic influences. This module will show how the two systems complement each other. They provide a complete view of a person's life path and potential.

Life Path and Sun Sign

Understanding your Life Path Number and Sun Sign is crucial in Astro-Numerology. Your Life Path Number, from your birth date, shows your true self and purpose. Your Sun Sign, based on your birth date, reveals your true self. It shows your outward expression, too.

Aries1: The Courageous Champion

Assertive, Bold, Direct, Determined, Courageous, Dynamic, Independent, Focused

Aries One (1) combines the Sun's fiery energy in Aries with the ambitious Life Path 1 in numerology, making you a real Courageous Champion. You excel in daring moves and favor forging your own path instead of conforming to tradition. You thrive on challenges and approach them with determination and courage to conquer them.

Straightforwardness and passion are important to you in your personal life. You wish a partner who mirrors your determination and intellect, and you're receptive to meaningful relationships when there's a strong connection. As a parent, you'll exemplify support and responsibility, instilling confidence and independence in your children.

Your professional strength lies in leading and innovating. Before finding your ideal career, you may experience multiple changes, but once you do, your innovative mindset and distinct abilities will drive you towards remarkable achievements.

You have a natural ability to lead and strong opinions, and you prefer taking direct action to achieve results. Your unique talent for innovative problem-solving differentiates you. When you adopt flexibility and foster meaningful relationships, your achievements become even more fulfilling.

Aries 2: The Diplomatic Warrior

Courageous, Gregarious, Headstrong, Argumentative, Inspired, Sensitive, Impulsive, Shy

Aries Two (2) merges the adventurous nature of Aries with the contemplative qualities of Life Path 2. You're a Diplomatic Warrior, driven by passion and guided by strong ethics. You seek to create a better world, finding a balance between adventure, achievement, and love. Regardless if it's a daunting endeavor or mundane responsibilities, you adhere to your own guidelines and remain faithful to your purpose.

Your love shines in relationships and you hold companionship in high regard. You desire a partner who comprehends and supports your goals, while also enjoying romance. Finding someone who meets these standards shows that you're prepared for a committed relationship.

Your professional strengths lie in leadership positions like CEO or manager. You are a trustworthy leader because of your knack for staying focused and completing tasks. You have a cautious approach to personal expenses and choose to invest in ventures that align with your values.

You thrive in positions that enable you to leverage your charm and leadership abilities to drive change. Trusting your instincts is important, but you find success by balancing bold actions and thoughtful consideration. Prioritise supporting and guiding others with your skills instead of overwhelming them.

Aries 3: The Practical Romantic

Assertive, Artistic, Arrogant, Cynical, Courageous, Imaginative, Excessive, Distracted, Creative, Romantic, Domineering, Extravagant, Enterprising, Sociable

Aries Three (3) combines charisma, humour, and never-ending vitality, reminiscent of Peter Pan. Your youthful heart and magnetic presence attract people, regardless of their age. Your life is brimming with lively experiences and exciting new adventures, and your friendships encompass people of all ages.

Your romantic inclination and belief in personal control drive you to accomplish remarkable feats. With vivid dreams as your driving force, you face obstacles head-on, constantly striving to achieve your goals. You thrive in the spotlight, thanks to your charm and imagination, as you enjoy being acknowledged and sharing your happiness with others.

In matters of the heart, you eagerly pursue fresh adventures-and readily develop feelings for potential partners. When it comes to romance, you bring enthusiasm and creativity, willing to go to great extents to win over your desired partner. If the feelings aren't reciprocated, you might lose interest fast, but once you're committed, you're steadfast and motivated.

You thrive in your career by being skilled in multiple areas. Your friends' network presents you with opportunities, and you excel at transforming ideas into actuality. When it comes to finances, you are generous and enjoy both making and spending

Your creativity and dedication will impress both artists and entrepreneurs. Your optimism and charm are great attributes, but staying focused and grounded will make your dreams come true. Achieve success by blending practical goals with the power to inspire and persuade.

Aries 4: The Practical Architect

Creative, Practical, Impulsive, Lazy, Courageous, Persistent, Naive, Too Busy, Enthusiastic, Organised, Domineering, Undemonstrative, Passionate, Traditional

A rare breed, an Aries Four (4) is both a visionary dreamer and a doer who brings those dreams to life. Unlike other Aries who may leave ideas unfinished, you actively pursue practical achievements and ensure their completion.

You have ambitious thinking but remain grounded, steering clear of impractical daydreams. When one idea doesn't pan out, you can apply your lessons to cultivate alternative opportunities. Even if they appear ordinary, you fill your life with thrilling adventures and unforgettable moments.

You remain young and curious in your mind, never aging in spirit. Your enthusiasm for each adventure is unwavering, regardless of whether your friends can keep up. You find excitement in the journey, even with knowledge of the destination.

Fairy-tale love stories are your specialty, and you desire for romantic narratives. Once the perfect partner comes along, you'll be prepared for a passionate and long-lasting relationship. Establishing marriage should provide stability while also allowing for individual freedom. Keeping the passion alive is crucial for your partner. Despite occasional thoughts of extramarital relationships, you value faithfulness and recognize the challenges it presents.

Money provides you with security and independence. Since you were young, you've strived for more than just a salary, pursuing tangible achievements like a prestigious position or financial prosperity. Your strength lies in roles that involve decision-making and procedure-setting. Although being in charge of your own business might be desirable, family duties often come first. Finding a balance between work and family is vital, and starting your own business could be the perfect solution.

It's difficult to discourage you, but pushing your limits can make it happen. Include downtime in your schedule and take time to relax, like going for walks and reflecting. Your determination and innovation propel you towards success and motivate those around you. Motivate others to believe in the impossible by sharing your achievements and difficulties.

Aries 5: The Creative Liberal

Creative, Communicator, Headstrong, Fickle, Generous, Freedom-Loving, Audacious, Careless, Bold, Energetic, Quarrelsome, Self-Indulgent, Pioneering, Resourceful

Aries Five (5) thrives on bold risks and innovative ideas, always leaping from one adventure to another. Your boldness to take risks stems from your vision for a better world. You're adept at discovering alternative paths and ideas, even in the face of obstacles.

You are a champion of personal freedom, opposing any sign of oppression. Your commitment to justice started early in life and has only strengthened, inspiring those around you with your persuasive ideas. Your thirst for knowledge is driven by curiosity, emphasising prizing embracing the present.

You prefer charm over confrontation, making risk-taking your signature style. Today's enemy could become tomorrow's friend, and you adjust despite occasional obstacles.

Seek a partner who respects your autonomy and has their own passions or professional goals. To you, marriage is more about having a supportive foundation than always being together. Even the romance can benefit from occasional separation.

Early on, you realise that money is synonymous with freedom for you. In management, it's preferable to delegate routine tasks in order to concentrate on impactful work such as networking and client interactions. If you enjoy exploration and variety, careers in journalism or communications are ideal for you.

You are exceptional at mentoring and challenging societal norms. Achieve effective leadership by maintaining balance, prioritising health, and using talents..

Aries 6: The Intrepid Idealist

Generous, Nurturing, Jealous, Self-Righteous, Ambitious, Responsible, Excitable, Nosy, Practical, Loyal, Sanctimonious, Obstinate, Constructive, Idealistic

Aries Six (6) is driven by the desire to educate and encourage, going to great lengths to unlock the potential of others. Lack of appreciation can lead to discouragement, but you're resilient and continue to persevere.

Balancing personal growth, romance, and achievement, your practical Renaissance-man approach shines. In order to: While working towards your own objectives, you have a firm commitment to assisting others. You balance a quick wit with caring attributes, mindful of your reputation and expecting others to do the same.

You are an exceptional parent and desire a cozy, love-filled home. Love and sex can be separate, but when they come together, it's a powerful experience. You believe in establishing a strong connection first before making any long-term commitments. It's essential to find a partner who holds the same values as you.

You strive for a luxurious lifestyle and put in dedicated effort to achieve it. Whether in HR, education, or the entertainment industry, you're dedicated to both excellence and long hours. Remaining loyal to your coworkers, it is difficult for you to part ways with those who depend on you, yet you flourish in the face of change and challenge.

With a caring and nurturing approach, you can deliver challenging news and lead with compassion. While you strive for harmony, you'll guard your loved ones. Be a role model as a leader and assist others in reaching their potential. The most valuable gift you possess is your faith in others, and the world's gift to you is unconditional love.

Aries 7: The Scientific Psychic

Assertive, Analytical, Arrogant, Aloof, Creative, Technical, Impulsive, Secretive, Passionate, Articulate, Jealous, Repressed, Enterprising, Perfectionist

Aries Seven (7), your true talents may not be obvious at first glance because you assess situations before taking action. You carefully assess situations before taking action, finding joy in the process and being motivated by data and strategy, sometimes valuing them more than the result. When you lose interest in a pursuit, you detach and leave others puzzled.

Through learning, you satisfy your adventurous spirit by delving into different fields with curiosity and precision. Whether it's learning to drive, love, or earn money, persistence is how you master new skills. Young Aries individuals gain the skill of selecting their fights, balancing emotions and strategic thinking.

Your interests in history, law, politics, and the mystical are captivating, and you delve into them. Your insightful nature leads to pleasant surprise when others surprise you.

Whether it's a memorable encounter or a shared intellectual bond, unique connections kindle your interest. For you, sex can encompass both love and presupposing thrill. You desire a partner who fulfils your intellectual and physical requirements. When you encounter the ideal match, you develop into a committed and imaginative partner.

Leading others is desirable only when they have a similar level of education and commitment. You show exceptional management skills in these cases, commanding respect and providing valuable training. Your financial behaviour is both thrifty and strategic, balancing occasional treats with secure savings.

You balance your work behind the scenes by sharing your scientific expertise. Despite your need for solitude, you share your expertise. With maturity, you could produce philosophical works, gaining insight from experiences that blur the lines of ethics. Cultivating your mind is the key to finding the wisdom you desire.

Aries 8: The Inspired Professional

Assertive, Capable, Impatient, Indecisive, Generous, Professional, Excessive, Workaholic, Enthusiastic, Open-minded, Headstrong, Money Problems, Creative, Sensuous

Aries Eight (8) - With your keen perception, you grasp that defining right and wrong can vary based on perspective. Just like Buddha, being an Aries Eight means you have a powerful drive to lead and advise others, making use of your deep understanding to make choices and move forward. Your balanced perspective on rewards and consequences makes you a trusted advisor, sought after for your fair counsel.

Tolerance is a value you cherish, and you reject rigid boundaries. By recognising that truth empowers, you remain open-minded and aim to guide others using your own experiences.

You desire a partner who complements you, shares your passions, and supports the household so you can focus on your career. Your perfect partner is someone who both contributes to the family budget and shares equal responsibilities in the relationship. In a partner, you desire someone who can keep up with your stamina and creativity, and enjoys both sensual pleasures and deep philosophical connections.

The aim in fields like law, politics, or finance is to make a meaningful difference and observe tangible results. You flourish in authoritative positions where you can guide and inspire others towards successful outcomes. Your finances may fluctuate, but you handle them through careful planning. You earn money as a reflection of your hard work and achievements.

A strong partnership often emerges when career and marriage have defined roles. Together with your partner, you can form a dynamic team and achieve brilliant success.

Your distinct perspective and commanding attributes empower you to lead varied teams and achieve meaningful outcomes. Striving for success and savouring life's simple pleasures, you balance hard work and enjoyment. As you progress in your career, you may switch directions but continue to be a valuable resource and friend to many. Embrace the equilibrium of the spiritual and physical dimensions, realising that desire alone cannot solve every issue.

Aries 9: The Enterprising Performer

Dynamic, Artistic, Impulsive, Charismatic, Creative, Compassionate, Moody, Inconsistent

From a young age, you've charmed and influenced others with your energy, Aries Nine (9). Your unique leadership style and approach draw in followers, but you're also quick to adjust when needed. Resilience and enthusiasm characterises your response to setbacks, as you seek out new challenges.

You are looking for a partner who possesses the same level of passion and adaptability. Despite the challenges, you fully commit and support in relationships and parenting.

Careers in entertainment, law, and business benefit from your dynamic approach. Your creative and energetic work brings stability, even in the face of initial financial obstacles. Your innate leadership and inspiration shine through as you navigate both personal and professional spheres, all while striving for authentic love and happiness. Achieve long-term fulfilment by embracing the present and staying focused.

Taurus 1: The Bold Builder

Ambitious, Decisive, Impatient, Industrious, Determined, Hot-tempered, Wilful, Jealous

Taurus One (1) - You embrace life with confidence, aiming for success and enhancing systems while upholding tradition. While you prioritise appearances and can be rigid, you pursue your goals and prefer to lead by example.

Although you may have many romantic entanglements, approach them with sincerity and commitment. Once you're comfortable, you exhibit possessiveness and intensity, but your passion often leads to conflict resolution and stronger connections.

You thrive in positions like CFO or image consultant, fuelled by power and authority. Your effective financial management and creative strategies enhance personal and professional prosperity.

While your self-confidence and leadership are assets, be careful not to become too inflexible. To build a successful and harmonious environment, remember to balance your drive with respect for others' perspectives.

Taurus 2: The Charismatic Challenger

Ardent, Accommodating, Slow-moving, Unassertive, Hospitable, Understanding, Complacent, Shy, Calm, Gentle, Over -deliberate, Sulky, Loyal, Modest

Taurus Two (2) - You have an adorable personality, finding a balance between socialising and enjoying cozy nights at home. You desire stability and offer it to others, but may appear demanding to independent individuals.

You appreciate lasting connections based on friendship and honesty, showing dedication and care. Despite being seen as accommodating, you desire a partner who values your sincerity and can handle the pedestal you place them on.

Your chosen careers show a passion for aiding and enhancing. Thriving in roles like diplomacy, acting, or design is a result of your exceptional sense of tact and taste. When you make your contributions visible and appreciated, your financial situation improves.

You show an example through your gentle and dependable personality. Your unwavering support and resilience make you an irreplaceable presence in others' lives, even if not always recognised.

Taurus 3: The Sensuous Charmer

Sensuous, Imaginative, Sensual, Trivial, Artistic, Debonair, Lazy, Dishonest, Buoyant, Carefree, Gluttonous, Dissipative Boisterous, Sociable

Taurus Three (3) - You possess a talent for theatrics and a contagious enthusiasm for living. Being in the spotlight is your thing, whether it's a family occasion or a whimsical daydream. Your charisma and talent make you the centre of attention at social gatherings, but achieving real-world success may be more challenging for you.

You crave beauty and elegance in life and love, seeking mental and emotional compatibility. Your perfect match should match your playful, high-energy lifestyle and also appreciate deep connections. Joy, imagination, and a love for extravagance and fun characterise your attitude towards sex.

Creativity and showmanship are essential for your career to flourish, whether it's in acting, writing, or any role that lets you entertain and captivate. You excel at attracting resources and financing your extravagant lifestyle, but it's crucial to balance your playful nature with practical endeavours for lasting success.

Your purpose is to bring excitement and style to everyday life, turning ordinary moments into unforgettable ones. Your enthusiasm and creativity have the power to improve any situation or relationship. To unlock your full potential, challenge yourself and follow your natural talents to reach your goals.

Taurus 4: The Constant Contributor

Stable, Hardworking, Rigid, Unimaginative, Patient, Traditional, Solid, Argumentative, Diligent, Persistent, Stubborn, Skeptical, Dependable, Constructive

Taurus Four (4) - From an early age, you loved to build. It didn't matter if it was toy trains or elaborate dollhouses. Your hands-on approach to life has only strengthened as you've matured, and you're probably the one who meticulously plans and carries out projects with precision and commitment.

You prioritise stability and loyalty in relationships, desiring a partner who is just as committed and reliable. When it comes to physical intimacy, you prefer it to be uncomplicated and sincere. Your approach to courtship and marriage emphasises practicality and long-term companionship rather than short-lived romance. Physical compatibility and a harmonious life rhythm matter to you, and you prefer straightforwardness over dramatic displays or complex relationship conversations.

Your meticulous and systematic approach sets you apart in positions that involve research, construction, or in-depth analysis. Engineering, architecture, and scientific research are ideal career paths for someone with your skills. Your talent for effectively organising and leading people makes you a valuable candidate for middle management roles that prioritise execution and dependability. Despite your preference for practical work, you demonstrate financial prudence by investing wisely and planning for the future.

In any setting, you are a crucial element that offers both stability and reliability. Nonetheless, be cautious of becoming overly rigid or complacent. While your commitment and concentration are admirable, infusing everyday life with joy and humour can enhance your encounters and connections. Embrace change and keep working towards a future that combines your practical strengths with some spontaneity.

Taurus 5: The Mischievous Master Builder

Elegant, Flexible, Greedy, Fickle, Self-reliant, Resourceful, Unfaithful, Reckless, Genial, Curious, Self-indulgent, Gullible, Decisive, Articulate

Taurus Five (5) - You're not one to shy away from change; in fact, you thrive on it. With an unyielding desire for new experiences and a love for exploring the world, you're in search of the next adventure. The way you blend unconventional and alluring elements in your style makes even the most boring tasks seem interesting.

It's common for romantic relationships with you to involve a lot of balancing. You desire a partner who can synchronise with your shifting moods and desires, respecting your need for independence. While you're open to relationships, you like to stay in control and maintain a tight grip on the reins. If you feel restricted, your desire for physical stimulation can cause cheating, but you view it to revive the primary relationship rather than endangering its stability.

With your physical grace and stamina, you're a perfect fit for careers that demand both strength and dexterity, like athletics, dance, or physical therapy. If you excel in strategic thinking and discipline, consider pursuing a career in the military or high-stakes journalism. Money is the means to attain a luxurious lifestyle, abundant in comfort and adventure. Your generosity often benefits friends, though you're aware of how they might take advantage of your kindness.

You are on a mission to prove that breaking conventions and maintaining integrity can go hand in hand. Despite your unpredictable behaviour, there is a stable core that keeps you grounded. Your self-assurance and willingness to take risks can serve as a source of inspiration for others, but it is crucial to use your abilities in a considerate and responsible manner. Balancing stability and change is key to reaching your goals and creating a lasting impact.

Taurus 6: The Sensuous Materialist

Loyal, Sensitive, Possessive, Opinionated, Responsible, Conventional, Covetous, Narrow-minded, Magnanimous, Loving, Conventional-minded, Down-to-earth, Pampering, Obdurate

Taurus Six (6) - You embody the essence of stability and nurturing. Regardless of your upbringing, you possess a natural bond with nature and a longing to establish a safe and cozy space for yourself and those you care about. The desire to ensure your family's well-being compels you to construct a stable groundwork, be it through traditional methods or by fashioning an extravagant sanctuary.

For relationships, you prioritise establishing a stable and long-lasting bond. Your preference is for a calm life with uninterrupted time spent with your partner. You focus your love style on touch and sensory experiences. To you, love means finding joy in life's simple moments as a couple, whether it's a fancy dinner or a cozy night in. Your commitment to your partner is strong, and you're willing to withstand any difficulties together.

Roles that combine friendliness and diligence, like management, executive positions, or arts-related roles, are where you shine. You excel as a team player because of your warm and responsible nature, although you may encounter challenges with delegating tasks because of your meticulous attention to detail. Careers that involve creating beautiful or functional things, such as fashion design, interior design, or real estate, are a great fit for you. You thrive in jobs that involve caring for and educating others.

Your beloved reputation among friends and colleagues stems from your genuine charm and dependability. You have high expectations for harmonious and comfortable living. Still, make sure not to get too comfortable or trapped in monotonous routines. Surround yourself with individuals who inspire and motivate you to reach new heights, preventing you from becoming complacent in your lavish surroundings.

Taurus 7: The Conceptual Conduit

Determined, Inventive, Stubborn, Choosy, Alluring, Analytical, Haughty, Aloof, Imaginative, Selective, Stingy, Introverted Commonsensical, Specialised

Taurus Seven (7) - You embody a fascinating blend of contradictions and complexities. You have a captivating and enigmatic aura, projecting intelligence and charm. This intriguing duality captivates others as they try to reconcile your sophisticated thinking with your captivating personality.

Your affectionate personality and independent streak can create challenges in your relationships. You approach love with a cognitive perspective, expressing your emotions through sensuality and physicality instead of overt declarations. You might face challenges with traditional commitment, resulting in unconventional arrangements like long-distance relationships or complex love triangles. If you discover a partner who aligns with your intellectual and emotional needs, you experience a fulfilling relationship that endures.

With your creative and analytical skills, you are a perfect fit for roles in the arts, invention, or product development. You possess a one-of-a-kind skill to transform ideas into prosperous ventures, whether through adding a distinctive touch to existing concepts or by integrating diverse elements into cohesive projects. Ideal careers include technical innovators and creative directors, where you can work and. Despite the potential for substantial riches, your ultimate contentment stems from the collection and presentation of rare, meaningful objects that mirror your discerning preferences and reserved disposition.

Imbuing ordinary things with a sense of wonder and enchantment is your life's goal. Unlocking the inherent value and beauty of everyday experiences is possible through your potential. Striking a perfect balance between analytical precision and warmth, your role model image is both inspiring and relatable. The power of your achievement in this endeavour lies in its ability to make you a beacon of hope and creativity, exemplifying the fusion of the practical with the extraordinary.

Taurus 8: The Empire-Building Executive

Determined, Capable, Materialistic, Workaholic, Unstoppable, Professional, Calculating, Driven, Imposing, Authoritative, Avaricious, Power-hungry, Steadfast, Ambitious

Taurus Eight (8) - You charted your course for success early on, driven by precision and determination. With your Taurus Eight characteristics, you possess a strong business acumen and excel in managing high-stakes situations and global matters. You may find yourself in positions such as CEO or international banker, where accumulating wealth and achieving status will come to you.

You ground and think carefully about your approach to romance, choosing a partner wisely and fully committing. While you may not always be emotional, your displays of love are extravagant and full of thought. Being possessive yet loyal, you might find yourself more drawn to fantasy than infidelity, and your strong work focus can limit your chances of romance.

You thrive in positions of wealth and power, like executive roles or consulting. Your home reflects your status, boasting valuable items and extravagant decor. You enjoy luxury but also seek value in your purchases.

Your determination sets you apart as a role model for achieving success. Realise your potential by finding a balance between material pursuits and spiritual development, without becoming too controlling. By engaging in philanthropy or mentorship, you can enhance your impact and enrich your achievements.

Taurus 9: The Ingenious Benefactor

Affectionate, Compelling, Indolent, Careless, Creative, Compassionate, Orthodox, Daydreaming, Purposeful, Spiritual, Smug, Self-interested, Unflappable, Generous

Taurus Nine (9) From a young age, you showed wisdom and kindness. You cared for the underdog and believed in everyone's potential. Openness characterises your spiritual beliefs, valuing personal experience and inclusivity more than rigid doctrine.

Love with you is a mixture of intensity and complexity. You feel "love at first sight" but may hold back certain parts of yourself. Your sensuality is captivating, but your afterglow may be more about moving on to your next fascination rather than lasting romance.

You have a talent for networking and persuasion, which makes you successful in roles that involve influencing and connecting with others, like ministry, journalism, or advisory positions. Your willingness to give away more money than you keep may impact your financial stability.

Your unique talent for inspiring and guiding others is a gift that empowers them to unlock their own strengths. Embrace who you are and use opportunities to reach your goals and create a meaningful impact.

Gemini 1: The Visionary

Congenial, Visionary, Resilient, Motivated, Independent, Protective, Intellectual, Versatile

Gemini One (1) is a sociable individual who values both a busy social life and alone time. Take advantage of this alone time to foster your innovative thoughts. Your special talent lies in navigating life's challenges, adjusting to unexpected changes while staying focused on your objectives. You excel in the future because of your unwavering determination and clear vision. You hold freedom as sacred, believing it should be a universal right and advocating for everyone's ability to express themselves and chase their aspirations.

For love, you want a partner who can match your intelligence and join in your adventures. Individuals who challenge your intellect and embrace exciting pursuing potential partners attract you. Although you cherish your independence, you desire a partner who can provide emotional and intellectual support. Once you discover your soulmate, your romantic nature blossoms, and you embrace the happiness of companionship.

Key factors for your success include your sharp memory, wit, and ability to engage in meaningful conversation. You are skilled in environments that appreciate adaptability and are unafraid to assume diverse responsibilities within a company. Although you don't prioritise wealth, you understand the value of financial stability and will explore opportunities that match your principles. Your ultimate aim is to discover a profession that lets you balance work and leisure, granting you the freedom to pursue your passions, such as opening an antique store or mastering a new craft.

You have a natural talent for generating ideas and bringing them to life. Your unique perspectives and extensive knowledge of human nature have positioned you as a respected individual within your social circle. Your ability to think, respond, and stay determined distinguishes you in any field. To reach your maximum potential, concentrate on forming strong teams, sharing your sense of humour, and staying genuine. Genuine success and fulfilment come from being true to yourself.

Gemini 2: The Ambidextrous Diplomat

Articulate, Patient, Adaptable, Supportive, Diplomatic, Gregarious, Thorough, Curious, Sensitive, Nervous, Argumentative, Scattered, Moody, Gossipy

Gemini Two (2) combines lively charm with cautious restraint. Your Gemini nature comes with the caution and selectiveness of a Two. You excel at being sociable while maintaining diplomacy, navigating social situations. Your complexity surpasses that of others, rendering you a captivating mystery. Like a clever chameleon, you adjust your outer persona to match your surroundings while safeguarding your true self. Only those who have earned your trust get to see the layers of your inner world.

Your ideal partner in love is someone who can keep up with your dynamic personality and match your intellectual curiosity. If you meet someone who pushes all the right buttons, you're not afraid to jump into a relationship. Your ideal partner is someone who accepts you as you are, joins you in adventures, and appreciates your unique qualities. Your unwavering loyalty is a beacon in this chaotic world. You uphold fidelity and cherish the sacredness of marriage, while also safeguarding your heart during challenging times. You choose to weather storms, but never distance yourself from loved ones.

The relationship between your finances and professional life is a classic case of duality. While you want financial security, you also enjoy spending on things that bring you happiness. However, you refuse to compromise your health for a demanding job. You excel in positions where you can manage projects, offer consulting services, or use your technical abilities without supervising others. Your happiness lies in being in charge of your work, be it in technology, teaching, diplomacy, or creative writing. You excel at maximising your resources and find a balance between income and lifestyle.

Gemini 2 excels in its capacity to maintain determination in challenging situations. You dedicate yourself to your responsibilities and put forth maximum effort in everything you do. You have the wisdom to exit situations that no longer benefit you, with no remorse. The most rewarding and challenging experiences for you come from close relationships. Connecting with others comes to you, but venturing into more meaningful conversations can be overwhelming. Trust your instincts and embrace genuine connections to experience the true fulfilment of relationships. Your success depends on your discretion, as well as your ability to learn and adapt. Your capabilities are greater than you think–you can accomplish your dreams.

Gemini 3: The Versatile Romantic

Vivacious, Artistic, Generous, Sociable, Imaginative, Restless, Indecisive, Extravagant, Distracted, Gossipy

Gemini 3: You're a romantic at heart. You dream of a perfect love story and wait for a big break in life. Despite setbacks, your resilient spirit helps you recover and move forward, complementing your stylish exterior. Variety fuels you, as you manage multiple projects, convinced that one will succeed. Your dynamic social circle results from your magnetic personality and the way you captivate others with your vibrant energy.

Love involves desiring both intellectual and physical connection. You long for a companion who has achieved great success, possesses remarkable intelligence, and eagerly seeks out new adventures. Your ability to see potential in relationships sets you apart as a visionary. Taking parenting means embracing the journey of raising children and treasuring them as grown-ups.

Your financial situation is just as unpredictable as you are—here one moment, gone the next. You always find solutions to financial challenges by thinking creatively. Your enemy is boredom. Each career choice is an opportunity to express your creativity, driven by passion instead of profit.

Your biggest strengths lie in your generous nature and appreciation for beauty. Your belief lies in spreading good fortune, whether it be through gifts, time, or a kind word. Maintaining focus can be difficult, but it allows your talents to shine brightly. Remember to first apply your light-hearted approach to yourself as the world needs it.

Gemini 4: The Inquisitive Realist

Clever, Persistent, Curious, Responsible, Practical, Gregarious, Restless, Contrary, Inconsistent, Verbose, Undemonstrative, Explorer, Capable

As a Gemini Four (4), you're a mix of stability and surprise. Your friends may assume your life is ordinary, but they're always surprised by your latest escapades. You excel in following a routine while always being ready to assist others, providing open-minded guidance and attentive listening.

You hold high standards for relationships. The ideal partner for you is someone who shares your love for travel and lifestyle. A healthy life is important to you and you seek a partner who feels the same. Your approach to sex is serious, and you value a strong mental connection to intensify the physical bond. Find a partner who balances practicality and dreaminess, grounding you without being controlling.

Your accountant often receives mixed signals as you try to balance comfort and security. You possess confidence in your skills and receive recognition from those in higher positions, but you may have alternate plans, such as launching your own business. You find equal enjoyment in both work and play, often blending the two together.

By engaging in leisurely pursuits, you continue to occupy your time, inspiring others to embrace adaptability and seek out new experiences. Aware of the challenges you've overcome, your friends truly appreciate your honest guidance. You are almost always accurate in your ability to assess people. Trust yourself and your journey, but pay attention to your intuition if something seems wrong.

Gemini 5: The Clever Communicator

Articulate, Resourceful, Intellectual, Versatile, Energetic, Inquisitive, Superficial, Restless, Manipulative, Impulsive, Fickle

Gemini Five (5) is a skilled communicator and networker. They connect with people and gather information. Your restlessness makes you want to explore unknown places and ideas. Your curiosity makes you a natural storyteller.

You're selective in love, seeking both intellectual and sexual compatibility. While cautious about commitment, you desire a soulmate, a home, and a family.

Routine bores you, and you'll have many career changes. You're drawn to public-facing roles in fields like marketing, entertainment, and journalism. Money is a means to live, but managing it can be a challenge.

You excel at connecting people and understanding trends. Finding an anchor–whether it's a family, business, or retreat–will help ground you and lead to the life you desire.

Gemini 6: The Free-Spirited Humanitarian

Articulate, Versatile, Gregarious, Idealistic, Responsible, Loyal, Possessive, Scattered

Gemini Six (6), you excel in both public and private settings, adapting. You have a strong inclination to seek wisdom from professionals and have a natural desire to assist others in enhancing their lives. Your true calling is teaching, using different methods to inspire and empower others.

In matters of love, you appreciate inner beauty, intelligence, and kindness and keep things private. Despite cherishing freedom, you find marriage to be more satisfying, as it offers the companionship and warmth you seek. Even though you may have doubts about being a good parent, you include children in your ideal family.

Although: According to your preferences, positions that empower you to teach, motivate, and engage with others are where your strengths lie. Regardless of your profession, the work you do has a lasting impact. Aiming to be a financial benefactor involves utilising resources and setting a positive example.

Finding balance is crucial for your success. Embrace help and prioritise both giving and receiving. You should acknowledge their unparalleled guidance and mentoring skills, but don't forget to celebrate their independence, even when they stumble. The world benefits from your wisdom and generosity, and your influence is profound.

Gemini 7: The Gregarious Scholar

Curious, Analytical, Witty, Perfectionist, Versatile, Detail-oriented, Private, Aloof

Gemini Seven (7) individuals, your curiosity has driven you. Since a young age, you've sought the strange. You've hunted for werewolves and dived into wizard tales. Your natural talent lies in piecing together unrelated information, making you intrigued by the unconventional. With such a broad range of interests, the opportunities ahead are boundless–whether it's pursuing academia or revolutionising the field of science.

Romance is an art form for you, often beginning with a organised secret rendezvous. Prioritising friendship is essential before contemplating marriage, and your ideal partner comprehends your perfectionist traits. When out in public, you look for someone who exudes grace and glamour, but in private, you prefer a partner who can alternate between intellectual collaboration and flirtatious seduction.

With your voice and intelligence, opportunities are just a step away thanks to your wide network. Despite your frequent placement in positions of power, you find satisfaction in quieter roles, such as medical research. Your approach to finances is cautious and discerning, with wise investments and discreet donations to causes close to your heart.

Your sharp insight allows you to see through lies, making you an expert in human behaviour. While you excel in logic, remember to embrace spontaneity in activities like visiting a museum or engaging in creative projects. Rely on your informed instincts and use your intelligence for the greater benefit.

Gemini 8: The Dynamic Executive

Versatile, Professional, Ambitious, Generous, Authoritative, Articulate, Global Perspective, Impractical, Indecisive, Workaholic, Materialistic

As Gemini Eight (8), you tackle every role with full dedication, from business to personal life. Once you decide, you commit and tackle many tasks with zeal. You lead a busy life, juggling event, planning and managing tasks, but you love the variety. During your occasional days off, you prefer to indulge in relaxation, such as rafting or traveling.

You consider marriage a sincere lifelong bonding. When joking around during courtship, we take the notion of "forever". Balancing work and romance can be tough, but having a partner who understands both is vital. Because of your loyalty and desire for genuine love, you refuse to marry for convenience.

Your strength as an executive lies in your ability to delegate tasks and foster team growth. You excel at recognising and maximising opportunities, with money not being your major priority. Recognition is important to you, and you will accept a lower salary for the chance to express your skills.

Your ability to see the bright side in tough situations is impressive. Your admirable optimism and effort are clear, even in the face of challenges that may not always lead to success. Make sure your schedule isn't overwhelmed and have faith in the sincerity of those around you. Combining your charm and positive attitude can lead to significant success in life.

Gemini 9: The Charismatic Explorer

Gregarious, Creative, Restless, Demanding, Open-minded, Compassionate, Superficial, Careless, Versatile, Impartial, Indecisive, Self-absorbed, Curious, Entertaining

Gemini Nine (9) - You have a strong desire for recognition and flourish under attention. The limelight beckons you, enticing you just like a moth to flame. The feeling of standing out fills you with energy and enthusiasm. In a crowd, your dynamic presence attracts notice and fuels your passion for the extraordinary. Whether you're in the spotlight or having a good time, you relish in being seen and bringing joy to others. Your enthusiasm leads you to explore new experiences, sometimes resulting in trouble. Despite everything, you are adept at bouncing back and moving ahead.

Like Auntie Mame, you embrace life as a joyful and educational adventure. Your heart is large, and you are willing to lend a hand to others. You possess both a curious nature, asking many questions, and a willingness to switch roles to offer support. Your dedication to fairness makes you a dependable friend and ally.

Casual flings aren't your thing. The search for depth and genuine significance drives our connections with others. Although your charm is attention-grabbing, what matters to you is finding a partner who comprehends and supports you, and who will share their life with you.

You don't enjoy traditional office jobs or managing others. Which do you prefer: working or leading a specific project? While your finances may be inconsistent, you are skilled at financing your escapades and assisting others. You see money to improve your life and differ for others.

Despite life's hardships, you continue to exhibit generosity, strength, and growth from your experiences. Remember to find a balance between your busy life and moments of solitude and family time. Make sure not to overwhelm yourself and find moments of relaxation to enjoy the simple things.

Cancer 1: The Determined Dynamo

Persistent, Original, Moody, Wilful, Understanding, Individualistic, Sullen, Know-it-all, Plucky, Gutsy, Passive, Blustering, Intrepid, Self-reliant, Aggressive

A Cancer One (1) refuses to accept a minor part. Your ambition pushes you to excel, but you prefer assertiveness over aggression. Your hard work may lead to success in the future, to create a comfortable life for you and your loved ones.

Although you may seem tough on the outside, you possess a sensitive and unpredictable nature. Others find it challenging to keep up with your shifting moods because your emotions clash with your logical side. Balancing societal expectations might be challenging as you seek outlets for both your caring side and assertiveness.

Anticipating the needs of your loved ones and caring for them is something you take pride in. You are a thoughtful partner who always remembers significant dates and makes extravagant gestures to express your love. Expecting others to understand your feelings without expressing them can cause misunderstandings. Offering a warm apology can help to reconcile after any conflicts.

Your deep emotional understanding makes you well-suited for creative fields such as writing and acting. Behind the scenes, you can excel in roles such as directing or producing. You excel at identifying opportunities and taking daring actions. You prioritise quality and will invest in it, but you derive more satisfaction from giving gifts than receiving them.

If you can manage your emotions as successfully as your professional responsibilities, you can achieve remarkable success. Entrust responsibilities and respect others' personal space. A remarkable ability to blend emotional care with practical effectiveness characterises your leadership. Opening up about your feelings allows others to gain insight from your rich emotional journey.

Cancer 2: The Conscientious Counsellor

Supportive, Emotional, Insecure, Intuitive, Considerate, Shy

Being a Cancer Two (2) means having a strong sense of empathy and intuition, often surpassing others in understanding their needs. Despite being nurtured, the influence of past slights can still affect your present. Learning your own needs and assert your independence is essential.

Misunderstandings can arise because of difficulty expressing emotions. Take the initiative instead of waiting for others. Avoid staying in unsatisfying relationships because of fear.

You have a natural inclination towards roles focused on justice and reform, like advocacy or psychology. You thrive in behind-the-scenes leadership and prefer staying out of the spotlight. As your confidence grows, you'll become more relaxed with money despite being cautious.

Prioritise your own needs and avoid taking things. Well use your insights and don't let others' problems overwhelm you.

Cancer 3: The Intuitive Optimist

Imaginative, Touchy, Well-intentioned, Defensive, Romantic, Talented

Cancer individuals with a Three (3) Life Path number personality have a knack for finding humor in the mundane, merging playful whimsy with a touch of classic elegance. You have a talent for transforming ordinary moments into entertaining stories and delivering clever one-liners. Your sensitivity leads you to be affectionate, although you stay shallow instead of going deep.

Your romantic nature is evident in your appreciation for grand gestures and thoughtful surprises. Despite occasionally going overboard, such as proposing with a surprise hidden in tacos, you have a playful side that shines through in your relationships. Your nurturing and joyful nature as a parent and grandparent shines through as you skilfully pamper and mentor your loved ones.

Given your distinctive style and humour, careers in the arts such as screenwriting or comedy suit you perfectly. Your talent in combining comedy and empathy makes you a great fit for writing or entertainment roles. Your Cancerian thriftiness doesn't prevent you from splurging on expensive things and pampering yourself.

The world becomes more vibrant with your whimsical viewpoint. Don't hold back your creative energy and allow yourself to indulge in what you love. Your one-of-a-kind viewpoint keeps you energetic and involved, enriching the lives of those in your presence.

Cancer 4: The Gentle General

Loyal, Persistent, Conservative, Comforting, Enterprising

A Cancer Four (4) is the dependable rock in everyone's life is a Cancer Four (4), even if they sometimes feel unappreciated. You're someone who values practicality and attention to detail, preferring organisation and security. After a tiring day, you find gardening or DIY projects to be relaxing because of their hands-on nature.

Your nurturing nature and emotional expressiveness shine through in relationships. Showing physical affection is important to you, and you may surprise your partner with a playful or unconventional touch. A sense of comfort allows your adventurous and playful nature to shine through.

Your strengths lie in jobs that prioritise structure and organisation, such as architecture or office management. You have a knack for being money-savvy with your practical approach to finances and finding bargains. You have a knack for wise investing and live a life of luxury without overspending.

Your honesty and dependability make you a valued friend and colleague. Despite occasional underestimation, never forget that you are the vital force that holds everything together. Everyone can always rely upon you as a crucial team member due to your practical skills and loyalty.

Cancer 5: The Hopping Homebody

Adventurous, Self-aware, Quick-witted, Free-spirited, Emotional

Cancer Five (5) possesses a balance between domesticity and wanderlust. Similar to a hermit crab, you're always on the lookout for fresh experiences and ideas, while also needing a comfortable home. The way you decorate your living space reflects your journeys and hobbies, with special keepsakes and a wide range of research resources.

In relationships, you seek a partner who has the same love for adventure and discovery as you do. Communication plays a crucial role in understanding. You're willing to revive your relationship with creative ideas, such as impromptu getaways or novel adventures.

Your ability to lead and motivate is outstanding, thanks to your creativity and Cancerian empathy. If you're interested in public relations, cultural anthropology, or travel and tourism, you'll thrive in careers that involve interacting with diverse cultures and ideas. You thrive in positions that allow for interpersonal connections and the display of your abilities.

Building connections comes naturally to you and people recognise you as a "people person."

Cancer 6: The Happy Homemaker

Tender, Domestic, Sentimental, Loving, Overprotective

Cancer Six (6) nature is all about nurturing and caretaking. Going above and beyond to take care of others, you create a secure and comforting place in your home where love and support are provided. Nurturing and safeguarding is your natural inclination, and you find happiness in household tasks such as cooking, cleaning, or gardening.

For relationships, you shine through with your dedication and loyalty, as you often commit for a lifetime. Your love is deep and unwavering, yet fear of rejection may hinder your ability to express your feelings. Your own gentle nature may be overshadowed if you are more assertive, attracting partners. Once you discover a compatible partner, your relationship has the potential to flourish by applying the lessons learned from previous experiences. Your longing for closeness and connection may lead you to be attentive, but it originates from a sincere desire to share every moment with your beloved.

You can apply your innate ability to create a nurturing home environment to careers that prioritise caring for and supporting others. If you have skills and passions in areas like cooking, real estate, healing, medicine, nursing, or teaching, these roles may be a good fit for you. You flourish in settings that enable you to interact with people and offer hands-on help. Working from home can be a perfect fit if you value personal interaction and community involvement, while also having family responsibilities.

Cancer 7: The Adorable Academic

Insightful, Psychic, Withdrawn, Caustic, Observant, Secretive, Poised, Shy, Dogmatic

Being a Cancer Seven (7) means you possess a unique mix of introspection and curiosity. Seeking understanding and connection is important to you, yet you often withdraw into solitude to recharge and introspect. Despite having a lively upbringing, your reserved demeanour may give others the impression that you are mysterious. The internal struggle between a deep emotional world and a need for privacy characterises your unique perspective on life.

When your desire for privacy and introspection clashes with your strong belief in traditional monogamy, it becomes difficult to find the perfect partner. In search of genuine connection? An affair might be the answer. If you don't reach out, even though you enjoy being alone, you can still experience deep loneliness. In relationships, you are caring and considerate, but also value personal emotional growth. Your sexual desire burns with an overwhelming passion.

Environments that foster creativity and introspection are where your career excels. Acting, singing, directing, producing, and writing are all natural ways to channel your talents. Although you seem laid-back, you have a powerful ambition and can be very strategic behind the scenes.

The way you balance innocence and sophistication is fascinating, showcasing both emotional and intellectual depth. This duality can be both intriguing and perplexing, both for yourself and those around you. Balancing your moods and introspection is key to staying connected with the people you care about. By finding equilibrium between your private world and your interactions, you can cultivate satisfying relationships and make the most of your profound insights.

Cancer 8: The Driven Delegate

Nurturing, Just, Possessive, Materialistic, Tenacious, Ambitious, Hesitant, Detached, Creative, Professional, Sensitive, Workaholic, Compassionate, Broad-Minded

The Cancer Eight (8) blend nurtures and has a powerful motivation. Your ability to understand the broader perspective, combined with your empathy, makes you influential. Success lies in finding a balance between your intense energy and powerful qualities.

Cancer 8's sensitivity and magnetism can be overpowering in relationships. Beneath your authoritative demeanour lies a profound emotional depth. Difficulty with trust and control can hinder partners from understanding your emotions. You can chase love with a fiery passion. Cancerian in you seeks courtship and commitment, while your Eight side seeks quick formalisation for goal-oriented focus.

Careers that blend empathy and strategic thinking, like marketing, promotions, or entrepreneurship, suit you well. Your ability to understand trends and pay attention to details make you well-suited for leadership positions. Stay away from mundane tasks or jobs that don't provide creative openings, as they might hold back your ambition and capabilities.

Overcoming a fear of success is a major challenge, but it's crucial for personal growth. Apply your wisdom for your own gain just as you do for others. Aim for a work-life balance and have confidence in your genuine motivations. Embrace your wide outlook and strive to support others while taking care of yourself.

Cancer 9: The Charismatic Creator

Receptive, Philanthropic, Self-Pitying, Self-Absorbed, Artistic, Spiritual, Reserved, Changeable, Compassionate, Magnetic, Self-Destructive, Melancholic, Sincere

Your Cancer Nine (9) sign exudes a captivating charm and a unique, imaginative perspective. You have an extraordinary talent for forming emotional connections, which makes you captivating and enjoyable to be around. You have a special talent for connecting with others, whether through humour or art.

Your character often displays extremes, as you oscillate between being a free spirit and a serene nature-lover. This duality can turn you into an intriguing parent or a quirky person, with unpredictable moments.

With your unique touch, you creatively and passionately infuse your romantic gestures, ensuring that they cherish and remember them. Marriage provides stability and a sanctuary from the world's chaos. Your kindness should be met with a partner who appreciates and reciprocates it, rather than someone who caters to your every desire. For relationships, you bring sensuality and playfulness, creating anticipation and joy in intimate moments. As a parent, you dedicate yourself to providing your children with both laughter and love.

You possess combine idealism and opportunism. You prioritise work that matches your passions instead of chasing money in your career. From the start, your involvement in creative projects is perfect for you because you excel at being an essential part of the process. It is clear that you drive success in ventures you are engaged in.

With your energy, your powerful presence and charm can truly make a difference, leaving people feeling inspired and entertained. It is vital to use your influence and refrain from exploiting your charm for selfish. Make it your goal to impact others with your vibrant personality.

Leo 1: The Misunderstood Monarch

Generous, Innovative, Conceited, Dictatorial, Passionate, Independent, Arrogant, Boastful, Noble, Bold, Status-Seeking, Impulsive, Dynamic, Original

As Leo One (1), you show the regal confidence and leadership of a lion. When you face challenges, you see the world as your personal stage. If the world disappoints you, you'll build a new one and excel in every role.

You display your talents and enjoy supporting others to reach their full potential while taking credit for it. You gravitate towards teaching and mentoring roles, embracing your natural leadership abilities and independent learning mindset.

Your romantic style is grand and dramatic, filled with extravagant gestures and planned dates. Although you have a commanding presence, you still seek reassurance and are conscious of how your partner views you. By being attuned to your partner's needs and desires, you can become a more focused and observant lover.

Parenting might bring you joy, but your youthful spirit and need for attention could make you view your children as competitors.

You have a natural inclination towards roles of leadership and artistic influence. To excel, you need a position where you can shine, whether it's leading a company, managing a fashion house, or influencing public opinion through the media. There's no denying your leadership skills, and you flourish in positions that grant recognition and influence.

Keep your guard up, as arrogance may be lurking nearby. It's important to have a circle of individuals who can offer honest feedback and listen to others. While you show excellence in various aspects, finding a balance between your achievements and humility is crucial for genuine connections and long-term prosperity.

Leo 2: The Valiant Valedictorian

Eager, Extroverted, Temperamental, Sly, Creative, Friendly, self-centred, Argumentative, Cheerful, Diplomatic, Childish, Hesitant, Warmhearted, Companionable

Leo Twos (2), you have a knack for tackling challenges with style. They are skilled at transforming challenges into chances, often benefiting from obstacles. You handle social dynamics thanks to Leo's resilience and the natural charm of the two. Your ability to think and your charm can disarm adversaries, but you choose compromise over conflict. When you've decided, you're resolute.

When you were young, you may have been the teacher's favourite, winning over your classmates with favours and witty remarks. By trying to please others, you have improved your skill in winning them over.

In relationships, you need continuous validation and praise. A need for reassurance accompanies your grand gestures and emotional expressiveness. To be suitable partners, they must be ready to meet your ego's demands and indulge your desire for affection. Being very demonstrative, you thrive on physical affection and constant reassurance of your partner's love.

In roles such as politics, entertainment, or high-profile positions, you possess innate qualities that make you a perfect fit for the spotlight. As a performer or spokesperson, your charisma and ability to captivate an audience make you stand out. Your talent for negotiation and self-promotion positions you as a successful leader or influential figurehead. Despite the weight of responsibility on your shoulders, you have an unwavering belief in your ability to make a positive impact on others.

Once you decide, your conviction remains unshakeable. When pressured, you might alternate between avoiding and assuming control. When acknowledged, even if you prefer to avoid being in the spotlight, your Leo traits come to life. Your ability to thrive in collaborative environments, where you provide support and uplift others, makes you a valuable asset as both a team member and a leader.

Leo 3: The Charisma King

Dashing, Generous, Flirtatious, Vain, Stylish, Fun-Loving, Inconstant, Garrulous, Entertaining, Spirited, Faddish, Cynical, Vital, Congenial

It's reassuring to imagine that, as the smooth talker, Leo Three (3), you had business cards ready from the start. The captivating nature of Leo Threes makes them capable of selling anything, but they prefer for only the finest. You were born to entertain and have the perfect host qualities: charming and always ensuring everyone has a great time. People recognise you for your extravagant gestures and luxurious style, which transform even the most modest gathering into a spectacular occasion.

Living a life full of intense attractions and dramatic relationships, you extravagant. You long for intense, all-encompassing passions, yet your constant need for admiration could make it difficult for you to maintain consistent relationships. Although monogamous, you struggle to stay committed because of your need for attention from multiple admirers.

Your strengths lie in positions that allow room for creativity and individual flair, rather than mundane responsibilities. If you enjoy working with high-profile individuals and have powerful skills in public relations and fundraising, these types of jobs are a perfect fit for you. Your natural talent for illusion and presentation is a perfect fit for industries like film, fashion, and the arts. You spark excitement and ideas. But your finances may suffer from your extravagant plans and love for indulgence.

You have an innate style and enthusiasm that make you shine like a star. No matter what anyone tries, you continue to be yourself. Embrace your identity as a dreamer and showman, but remember to steer clear of mere sensationalism. Keep showing off your assets and enjoying your abundant appeal and charm.

Leo 4: The Hail-Fellow Hercules

Loyal, Accomplished, Pompous, Exacting, Lusty, Strong-Willed, Show-Offish, Contrary, Jovial, Committed, Pushy, Dogmatic, Enterprising, Strong Values

Leo Four (4), you possess the aristocratic essence blended with the heart of a commoner. You see no task as too small and value people based on their character, not their status. A special mix of straightforwardness and regal composure makes you distinctive in any environment. Incredible determination and almost superhuman energy allow you to maintain high standards while staying relaxed when you're comfortable.

Combine dedication and determination for relationships. You have a firm commitment to success, tackling challenges with optimism and emotional engagement. You refuse to accept failure and would rather take the blame than admit to being wrong. Your practical understanding of human flaws tempers your romantic idealism, resulting in a balanced approach to love.

Your impressive work ethic propels you to excel and attain top positions. You have a natural talent for managing both people and finances. Despite being a demanding authority figure, your commitment to productivity and efficiency is commendable. You're well-suited for a role that blends practicality and beauty, such as horticulture. You love being in the center of attention, especially when it coincides with your work.

Mixing your Leo enthusiasm and persistent nature is unbeatable. Conventional standards consider you a hero, demonstrating exceptional effort and devotion. Stay alert and mindful of others, valuing their viewpoints. Embrace being a silent hero. But, remember that everyone, even the most remarkable people, has flaws. That includes you.

Leo 5: The Zany Zealot

Magnetic, Free-Spirited, Impetuous, Self-Indulgent, Courageous, Peppy, Hotheaded, Hasty, Exuberant, Communicative, Ostentatious, Undisciplined, Expansive, Resourceful

Being a Leo Five (5), you seek adventure and excitement to keep life interesting. You possess the same talent as Mick Jagger for embracing a fast-paced lifestyle and making every second matter. You love being the center of attention and breaking the rules, whether it's through elaborate storytelling or shocking others.

Just like your personality, your love life is full of excitement. You're always seeking more and more excitement, causing your romantic experiences to resemble a thrilling rollercoaster journey. You desire partners who can match your need for dramatic affection and passionate adventures. Your enemy is a monotonous routine. Despite your wild side, you possess a captivating energy and charm that draws people in.

You're attracted to attention and excel in creative and extravagant endeavours. You're not cut out for a mundane, traditional office job. If you desire freedom and visibility, freelancing or public-facing roles are ideal for you. You could have a job that puts you in the spotlight, but prioritising seeking thrills may be more important than managing your image and money.

You challenge norms and foster liberation in others. By embracing authenticity and inspiring others to break free from their routines, you empower people to embrace their wild side. While you may enjoy playing the role of a rebel, deep down, you want to inspire and uplift others. Your boundless energy and zest for life serve as a driving force for change, encouraging others to unleash their inner party animal.

Leo 6: The Humane Humorist

Loving, Home-Loving, Vengeful, Jealous, Faithful, Protective, Domineering, Overprotective, Magnanimous, Responsible, Overbearing, Self-Righteous

As a Leo Six (6), your sense of pride extends beyond yourself to your family and loved ones. Your warm and unwavering presence draws others towards you, making you a cherished ally and a powerful defender. Your inherent charm and charisma, along with your unwavering sense of morality and nobility, make you attractive.

You are an enthusiastic and committed partner who approaches relationships with passion. By being willing to commit, you may jump into love without considering compatibility. Despite this, you are an amazing partner because of your dedication and nurturing nature. Your expectations for yourself and others, especially regarding family, are very high. You balance affection and discipline in your home life, imparting strong values to your children while helping them navigate life's challenges.

Your ability to entertain and captivate is exceptional, in roles that require humour and performance. With your creative talents and meticulous attention to detail, acting, writing, and directing are a natural match for you. You could consider opening a restaurant or a similar business that combines your affinity for hosting and socialising with your professional life.

Your wide range of interests motivates you to explore various creative avenues, ensuring a sense of engagement and fulfilment.

You have a destined role to play in life as a hero, providing support, protection, and guidance to those in your circle. The way you blend unwavering principles, emotional depth, and humour ensures a long-lasting effect, whether in personal or professional settings. Your devotion to your loved ones and your ability to find joy in tough times will cause respect and admiration. Embrace your role as a guardian and provider, and you'll see that people appreciate your contributions, even if they don't always recognise them.

Leo 7: The Free-Thinking Trailblazer

Aristocratic, Reforming, Standoffish, Aloof, Alluring, Erudite, Arrogant, Repressed, Gallant, Dignified, Demanding, Inconsiderate, High-Minded, Articulate

Individuals born under the Leo Seven (7) sign possess a unique combination of sophistication and introspection. Your charm exudes a regal aura, and your intellect runs deep. You prioritise high ideals and introspection. People may perceive you as distant or disconnected. Behind a mask lies a profound inner world and a search for purpose.

In relationships, commitment is what you seek. Yet, the idea of losing your independence is a concern for you. Your ideal partner must adhere to demanding expectations. They deal with your occasional detachment. Your emotions may blaze fiercely at first, but then retreat when the relationship starts to suffocate. Selectivity and discernment characterise your romantic approach, aiming for a blend of passion and freedom. For a partnership to be fulfilling, it requires someone who respects your need for personal space. They should aim to captivate your intellect and emotions.

Your career path is driven by a desire for intellectual stimulation and personal growth. Roles involving exploring human behaviour, like therapy or social work, might suit you well. You are a perfect match for demanding and contemplative roles due to your strong analytical skills and empathy. Acting, music, or composing are vibrant fields where you can discover immense satisfaction and exhibit your artistic prowess. If you're into tech and innovation, you might enjoy this too. They occupy roles that provide them with constant learning opportunities and new challenges.

Your determination to better yourself is impressive. Your dedication to personal growth makes you a role model to many. Embrace your true self and leverage your insights for the benefit of others. Your personality and physical appearance can contribute to your professional achievements. However, it is important to combine your thinking skills with a proactive approach to life. By utilising your analytical and introspective skills, you can tap into your potential. They have the power to inspire and start positive transformations.

Leo 8: The Entertaining Entrepreneur

Self-Confident, Authoritative, Self-Involved, Overpowering, Commanding, Insightful, Intolerant, Bossy, Competitive, Capable, Intractable, Workaholic, Direct, Sensuous

Being a Leo Eight (8), your presence commands attention and respect. You possess the qualities of a born leader: confidence, assertiveness, and a sharp intellect that keeps you ahead of the game. When you speak, negotiate, or decide, you exude authority and expertise, making a lasting impact.

In love, you bring the same level of intensity and focus as you do in other aspects of your life. You have a calculated and efficient approach to seeking a partner, motivated by a hunger for stability and control. However, your inclination towards romance may overlap with your professional and personal worries. If other areas of your life are chaotic, it can affect your ability to commit to a relationship. Your love life can reflect your overall life situation, making it challenging to prioritise romance when there are unresolved issues elsewhere.

A powerful ambition for control and achievement shapes your work trajectory. You excel in positions that involve leadership and impactful decision-making, often choosing entrepreneurial ventures or leadership roles over conventional paths. Your talent spotting and development skills make you a skilled negotiator and business strategist. High-stakes settings are where you can shine, using your abilities to climb the corporate ladder or create a prosperous business. In managing a team, running a business, or negotiating deals, your direct approach and competitive nature set you apart and led to impressive success.

Your unmatched tenacity and resolve enable you to thrive in challenging environments and achieve outstanding success. Even though you might appear stern or commanding, your true intention is to excel and inspire others. Embrace your inherent leadership qualities and employ your keen insights to steer yourself and others towards novel opportunities. Your story is a testament to resilience and accomplishment, showing that with enough motivation and ambition, one can overcome challenges and achieve ultimate success. Always remember to maintain a balance between pursuing power and building meaningful relationships, so that a sense of fulfilment and collective success accompany your achievements.

Leo 9: The Lively Luminary

Charitable, Bombastic, Chameleon-like, Chivalrous, Outgoing, Egotistical, Careless, Dramatic, Magnetic, Extravagant, Possessive, Enthusiastic, Daring

The Leo Nines (9) have a natural talent for captivating and entertaining audiences. It is remarkable how you have an unmatched ability to make everything feel grand and dramatic, whether you're in the spotlight or working behind the scenes. Your ability to uplift others is undeniable, and you see yourself as a performer with a divine purpose, showcasing your undeniable charm.

Your magnetic personality will make you incredibly appealing in relationships, but your partner needs to be prepared for the admiration you attract. To complement your generous and loving nature, you need a mate who understands your need for attention and your occasional desire to be the centre of the universe. Your strong passion makes you appear demanding, and you have a tendency to be possessive and dramatic. Your kindness radiates even in the face of self-doubt. Pursuing something thrills you, but feeling too restricted may lead you to desire freedom. Once you calm down, you stay loyal and committed, even if your irresistible charm catches the eye of others.

Performance and public visibility will play a major role in your career. You excel as a chairperson, whether on stage or behind the scenes. You excel at controlling and guiding events, flourishing in positions that enable you to channel your artistic and theatrical talent. Your drive to be noticed and valued is clear in various aspects of your career, including acting, directing, and other prominent roles. Your valuable asset is your ability to captivate and inspire, making you sought-after in professions that value charisma and showmanship.

You exude an interesting combination of seductiveness, intellect, and spirituality. This blend carries a weighty obligation to employ your abilities for the benefit of others. Your natural inclination is to assist others and leave a positive impact. Your passion for environmental and social issues shows a firm commitment to creating significant global change. Despite your awareness of your exceptional abilities, you remain modest, understanding that your talents are most valuable when used to help others. Your dedication to education and inspiring others, combined with your deep environmental values, makes you a potential leader in environmental efforts for a better future.

Virgo 1: The Gymnastic Genius

Organised, Inventive, Petty, Cynical, Industrious, Straightforward, Fastidious, Contrary, Bright, Focused, Hypercritical, Inflexible, Health-conscious, Self-willed

Virgo Ones (1) exemplify both physical and mental discipline, blending a strong dedication to fitness with a keen, analytical intellect. Whether it's a challenging workout or solving complex problems, you approach everything with dedication and precision. Often, your dedication to having a flawless body conceals deeper insecurities, and you might rely on your physical achievements to create a perfect self-image.

In relationships, you expect a partner who matches your high standards in both intelligence and physical appearance. Like your workouts, you approach your love life with discipline, striving for perfection, and maintaining order. Your private life might be different from your public persona, showing a side of you that is passionate. You appreciate a partner who shares your enthusiasm and intellect because effective communication is important to you in the bedroom. Despite your reserved demeanour, you are adventurous and invested in the relationship.

You have the motivation to succeed and feel a strong sense of duty in your career. Your capabilities are impressive, as you consistently adapt and demonstrate resourcefulness, often taking charge of projects and initiatives. Your physical strength and discipline make careers in fitness, such as being a trainer, athlete, or dancer, a perfect fit for you. With your intellectual curiosity, you are well-suited for roles in publishing, advertising, or any field that requires meticulousness and organisation. Driven by a desire to be the best, you possess the ability to promote yourself and your ideas.

The potent fusion of physical vitality and mental agility is embodied in you. As a role model and perfectionist, your commitment and high expectations inspire others. Recognising that imperfection is a natural part of being human can increase your relatability and effectiveness as a leader. By embracing the balance between your disciplined exterior and authentic self, you and those around you can achieve greater success.

Virgo 2: The Consultative Consultant

Decorous, Sincere, Insecure, Shy, Thoughtful, Conscientious, Finicky, Argumentative, Concerned, Gracious, Negative, Self-conscious, Service-oriented

Virgo Twos (2) are introspective and detail-oriented. They often get lost in the minutiae of their thoughts and experiences.

Your habit of recording and reflecting shows a rich inner world. Others may not always see it. You may seem reserved or self-effacing. But you have a deep understanding of life that sets you apart. Your caution and attention to detail mask a vibrant, nuanced mind.

In relationships, your sensitivity and fear of hurt can create a complex dynamic. You may seem self-reliant, but your true self is more fragile and in need of genuine connection. Your tendency to second-guess yourself and your partner can lead to a cautious approach to love. You yearn for closeness but fear disappointment. Your dedication to your partner is strong. You seek a secure, appreciative, and harmonious relationship.

Supporting others and ensuring that systems run is often the centre of your career. Your empathy and problem-solving skills make you excel in mediation, healing, or coaching roles. You are well-suited for careers in alternative medicine or counselling. They involve helping others overcome challenges. Your analytical skills help you handle data. You can optimise processes and improve efficiency. You're also skilled at managing resources and helping others achieve their best potential.

To realise your potential, it's important to embrace your own worth and allow yourself to benefit from your hard work. Trusting your abilities and building self-esteem can help you. It will improve your relationships and help you achieve your goals. Your gift for empathy and compromise is formidable. With self-acceptance and confidence, it can inspire others to reach their potential.

Virgo 3: The Juggling Wizard

Practical, Optimistic, Critical, Boastful, Meticulous, Sociable, Fussy, Extravagant, Logical, Creative, Judgmental, Unstable, Idealistic, Expressive

The Virgo Threes combine methodical thinking with a vibrant and imaginative character. Although you have many ideas and may appear unfocused, your creativity and humour make things intriguing. You are both engaging and dynamic because of your skill in balancing detail and playfulness.

In a relationship, you merge witty banter with lighthearted teasing. Though you may appear reserved, your three qualities enable you to navigate romantic difficulties with humour. You invest time in finding the ideal partner, and once found, you show your love through imaginative and heartfelt gestures.

Your problem-solving skills and charm stand out in your career. Roles that require precision and creativity, such as editing or project management, suit you well. From a financial standpoint, you may find it challenging to strike a balance between saving and spending, pondering whether to purchase practical or indulgent items. While you may treat yourself sometimes, you maintain a frugal lifestyle.

You have a knack for linking people and ideas. Embrace your role as a bridge builder, accepting people for who they are without attempting to alter them. Your ability to blend practicality and creativity adds an interesting and balanced touch to your life.

Virgo 4: The Tactical Technician

Practical, Methodical, Humble, Unimaginative, Discriminating, Organized, Hypochondriacal, Reserved, Precise, Practical, Mechanical, Overcommitted, Modest, Principled

Virgo Four, you are the reliable problem solver and person people turn to for handling mundane tasks. Roles that demand precision and repetition, such as bookkeeping, repairing, and troubleshooting, are where you thrive. Perfection is your goal, and you understand that practice and careful attention to detail, while valuing time, are essential.

Your meticulousness could make you appear conventional, masking your inner emotions. Recognition for your work, like managing bills, driving carpools, or coaching teams, is something you appreciate. As you cultivate your relationships, incorporating some spontaneity can maintain the excitement. Your libido remains stable, and you approach sex with vigor and dedication, considering it a natural part of life.

Your expertise in hands-on work and meticulousness make you a perfect fit for technical or artistic roles. Precision and persistence are crucial qualities in careers like computer tech, dressmaking, or contracting. Even if creativity isn't your strong suit, your reliability and attention to detail make you an important team member. You find satisfaction in middle management, adding value without seeking recognition.

You aid others in valuing the little things and acknowledging advancement through baby steps. Your meticulousness and focus can help others, especially if you reduce criticism. Making a positive impact and improving the world is possible by embracing your strengths and practicing kindness.

Virgo 5: The Champion Cheerleader

Perceptive, Versatile, High-strung, Impatient, Eloquent, Active, Compulsive, Sharp-tongued, Cultivated, Quick-witted, Mercurial, Reckless, Erudite, Energetic

Virgo Fives are like adventurous youngsters who left home early in search of thrills. While they may have broken a few rules, their authentic nature is clear in their acts of giving. With a relentless desire for new experiences, they often find themselves in challenging situations that fuel their drive to excel.

Your powerful emotions and ability to detach can lead to dating multiple people or having many affairs. You may rationalise it as unimportant, but you alternate between intense joy and guilt. Your preference is for a partner who can keep up with your energy levels and fulfils your powerful need for physical affection. Domestic tasks may become more enjoyable than expected. Despite not being a born parent, you will make a wonderful friend to your kids, encouraging their curiosity and embracing their interests.

Your sharp wit and knack for networking, paired with Virgo's stability, turn you into an exceptional motivator and entertainer. You possess the power to motivate and energise individuals regarding their work. If you struggle with maintaining patience, you excel in dynamic positions like advertising or magazine editing. When the job piques your interest, you become a diligent worker.

You stand out and inspire others with your energy and charm, encouraging them to be themselves and excel. You assist individuals in escaping conformity, making the world a more captivating place. Keep in mind that not everyone will reciprocate your enthusiasm, and that's fine. Valuable perspectives can come from even those who adhere to the status quo.

Virgo 6: The Habitual Helpmate

Dutiful, Truthful, Nitpicking, Hypersensitive, Trustworthy, Obliging, Meddling, Outspoken, Honest, Kind, Crabby, Complaining, Respectable, Responsible

Virgo Six is a traditional helper, although to their detriment. Your commitment to helping others may sometimes seem excessive. Motivated by your own insecurities, you often push your loved ones to seize opportunities and excel. Criticising others may reveal your own insecurities about your worthiness.

While being well-intentioned in relationships, you take your sense of duty to the extreme. Being needed is often more important to you than being wanted. You may have a tendency to attract partners who are dramatic or unreliable and depend on you to bring out their hidden emotions. When you prioritise others too much, you may neglect self-reflection and assessing your partner's compatibility.

Your goal is to create a positive change in the world. While you may find satisfaction in a simple life, you also aspire to create a positive change in the world. You could consider pursuing careers in charities, education, medicine, or arts. For those who enjoy hands-on tasks, horticulture or catering could be attractive choices. Your desire for idealism compels you to seek purposeful work, even if it entails becoming an unsung hero.

Lofty expectations accompany your exceptional taste and wisdom for yourself and your loved ones. Finding a balance between responsibility and self-care is crucial, and remember that you don't have to deal with everything by yourself. Seeking help can be a constructive move—just avoid overwhelming guidance.

Virgo 7: The Academic Aesthete

Refined, Knowledgeable, Pedantic, Detached, Patrician, Truth-seeking, Over-analytical, Secretive, Orderly, Dignified, Supercilious, Suspicious, Self-controlled, Scholarly

Virgo Seven lives within an intellectual stronghold constructed during childhood. The allure of your detached demeanour captivates people, enticing them to unravel the mystery behind your composed exterior. While you appear self-sufficient and organised, you are also introspective, delving into your innermost self. It may seem snobbish, but deep down, you are democratic.

You might not be interested in traditional roles as a mate or parent. Your comfort lies in virtual connections rather than face-to-face interactions. The appeal of physical touch does not differ from your fascination with a bound book. You maintain control in your relationships and keep romantic partners distant. For finding love, you have your own approach. One may select tumultuous companions while longing for their liveliness.

You have a talent for excelling in freelance or work-from-home jobs. Use technology to create a personal workspace separate from your everyday routine. Solving complex problems and analysing behaviour is something you enjoy. Mystery writing, troubleshooting, computer programming, psychiatry, philosophy, or the arts are all careers that would be a good fit for you. You don't prefer manual labor.

You might have blind spots and be resistant to change, despite your sharp intellect. Take a step back from your daily routine and view yourself through the eyes of others. Engaging in regular meditation can bring calmness to your busy mind. Don't forget to communicate your emotions while sharing the gift of serenity and concentration with others. Inviting people in now and then can be beneficial.

Virgo 8: The Organised Operator

Disciplined, Poised, Obsessive, Intense, Clear-thinking, No-nonsense, Overemotional, Overstraining, Self-reliant, Efficient, Fastidious, Indecisive, Shrewd, Global view

Being a Virgo Eight, you're not inclined towards the rat race. Effective manoeuvring, not direct confrontation, ensures your security. People respect and admire your authority and competence because of your innate talent for balancing budgets and commitments. Your humility shines through in your community and business endeavours.

Love is often cast aside in favour of work, leaving it abandoned and forgotten. You're not the person who enters relationships or deals with messy breakups. Rather, you lean towards stability and may even insist on a prenuptial agreement. Finding the right partner means being willing to fight for the relationship with determination. Balancing your personal and professional worlds, your romantic life remains intense but private.

You have exceptional business acumen. A top executive role would suit you, allowing you to be part of a team while having autonomy. You have a powerful ability to lead your department and can resolve issues in other domains. Advancing your career involves working with a long-range vision, making calculated and well-thought-out risks. Even if one deal doesn't work, you're prepared with other options.

Your impressive ability to understand the overall picture and remain composed in stressful situations is admirable. You refuse to compromise your convictions or the convictions of others in order to belong. Your presence exudes a perfect blend of sophistication and approachability, commanding both respect and admiration. Often, in positions where you are regarded as a role model or face criticism, you demonstrate your dignity and conviction, imparting valuable lessons of perseverance and integrity to others.

Virgo 9: The Versatile Visionary

Cultured, Imaginative, Nervous, Critical, Respectful, Spiritual, Reticent, Unsympathetic, Dedicated, Entertaining, Fussy, Bitter, Thorough, Careless

Your ability to choose the perfect moment for impact is a characteristic of being a Virgo Nine. Since a young age, you have amazed and impressed others with your ability to exceed expectations. You possess a talent for crafting illusions with a hint of magician's flair, impressing that you are doing or saying the opposite of what you mean. Your talent for entertaining and love for living shines through in your ability to host events or run a restaurant, where you can showcase your wisdom and charm.

Your skepticism extends to marriage and parenthood, as you often question the validity of monogamy and the practicality of raising children in a troubled world. Yet, these worries are a disguise for real reservations. Before getting into a deeper relationship, you prefer to establish a strong friendship, showing your selectiveness in partner choice. Your inclination to remain friends with former partners showcases your skill in nurturing meaningful connections.

You are a trustworthy and interesting figure because of your calming presence and empathetic nature. People with this innate talent for connecting with others are a great fit for careers like psychologist, trial lawyer, or talk-show host. As a medical professional, you excel by blending compassion and objectivity, making you an exceptional surgeon. Acting, entertainment, or any role that involves interacting with others, such as being a nightclub entertainer or restaurateur, allows your dramatic and witty personality to shine.

Your warm nature makes you very likable. You are the perfect person to confide in, as you connect with others. Your playful wit contrasts with your stylish look. You have a knack for addressing insecurities with a touch of psychic insight. Embracing your intuition can help you overcome self-doubt. It will boost your already impressive versatility and charisma.

Libra 1: The Active Artiste

Polished, Innovative, self-centred, Glamorous, Trendsetting, Underachieving, Domineering, Attentive, Energetic, Self-absorbed, Flashy, Stylish, Assertive

Even without conventional attractiveness, Libra One possesses a captivating charm that attracts people. The desire to better oneself and one's surroundings might come across as superficial. Yet, it's about displaying your finest qualities.

Your ability to influence others comes naturally, with little effort. Instead of confrontation, you persuade people using your charm and charisma.

When it comes to relationships, you are an alluring partner who places importance on balance and equality. You value the importance of settling down, yet you perceive it as another duty to complete. You enjoy talking about issues instead of getting into arguments. As you grow older, you start to value deeper connections, but you still appreciate style and appearance.

Your skill in creating and presenting images suits you for careers in fashion, cosmetics, photography, or politics. You excel in roles that involve managing public perception and power. Enjoying luxury and spending money reflect your view of success and status.

You have a knack for adapting to trends and making connections. This skill helps you network and start new projects. You know many people. But deeper relationships will bring you more joy. Your charm can open doors and create opportunities. But, you must balance it with meaningful connections.

Libra 2: The Deft Diplomat

Balanced, Diplomatic, Vacillating, Indecisive, Well-mannered, Sociable, Inactive, Timid, Prudent, Companionable, Overdependent, Quarrelsome, Adaptable, Compassionate

As a Libra Two, you have a natural charm and grace, excelling in diplomacy and a sense of justice. You excel at finding compromises. You make others feel gratified. In disagreements, you prefer a gentle touch. You offer solutions that feel collaborative.

You're an excellent listener, which makes you a desirable partner. To be happy, you need a relationship where both partners are equal and sensitive. You may fear losing your identity in a relationship. So, it's vital to find a partner who is practical and understands your needs. You tend to be quite dependent, which can sometimes lead to co-dependence. You cherish the small details of dating and relationships.

You see your career as a stage where you play various roles, like an actor, politician, or ambassador. You're best at working behind the scenes rather than dealing with direct conflicts. Careers in the arts or sports might suit you. They would let you express your emotions and use your nervous energy. You value a nice work environment. You enjoy adding personal touches to your space.

Embrace action and make decisions. Your desire for fairness can sometimes cause you stress, as the world isn't always fair. Focus on areas where you can make a difference and focus on what makes you happy. Taking initiative and making choices will help you. It will balance your needs with others, fostering mutual understanding.

Libra 3: The Inspired Socialite

Convivial, Social-climbing, Scatterbrained, Suave, Artistic, Easy-going, Fickle, Flirtatious, Gracious, Superficial, Sycophantic, Discriminating, Romantic

As a Libra Three, you shine in social settings, dazzling others with your charm and style. You have a talent for networking and a deep appreciation for beauty and luxury. You love high society and glamorous lifestyles. You're often captivated by the wealthy and famous. Although you may not admit it, you enjoy keeping up with the latest gossip and social trends.

In romance, you embrace the fantasy of courtly love. It adds a touch of old-fashioned glamour to modern relationships. Your ethereal charm attracts admirers, and you enjoy being the center of attention. Your romantic approach may seem whimsical. But, it adds a magic to your interactions.

You prefer careers that allow you to be around beautiful things and people. You would excel in acting, fashion, or interior design. So would a job as a celebrity biographer or gossip columnist. Your drive for success often stems from a desire to enjoy and share luxury. You might even find fortune through connections or inheritance.

You excel as both a host and a guest, bringing elegance and flair to any event. Don't limit your talents to social circles; use them to create beauty and harmony in meaningful ways. You can organise charity events or share insights on celebrities. This can meet your love for the finer things in life. It can also make a real impact.

Libra 4: The Practical Dreamer

Persuasive, Stable, Waffling, Lazy, Discerning, Diligent, Mooching, Contrary, Even-tempered, Ethical, Manipulative, Too-busy, Equitable, Systematic

Libra Four, you handle many tasks with ease. You manage busy phone lines and demanding family members. You stay calm in the chaos. Even in the middle of pandemonium, you remain composed. You exude grace and tranquilly. You assess your possibilities and adopt a judicious viewpoint. Sometimes you avoid problems in order to safeguard your interests. You look determined, but you are adept at handling a lot of big, contradictory issues.

In relationships, you maintain a practical approach. While you can experience intense passion, don't let it disrupt your daily life. You are loving and sincere but dislike playing games or being unavailable. Instead, you prefer honesty and straightforwardness.

You excel at teamwork, setting a powerful example for others. In leadership or creative roles, you use Libra charm and practical Four traits to succeed. Your work is stylish and accessible. Your critical eye helps in science and sports. You handle challenges with both wit and determination.

With a mix of Libra charm and Four practicality, you can soar. Your calm, balanced nature sets a good example. You will guide and support others through life's difficulties.

Libra 5: The Global Glamour-Puss

Social, Easygoing, Inconstant, Unfocused, Witty, Versatile, Frivolous, Self-indulgent, Fluid, Alert, Shallow, Discontented, Fluent, Vivacious

As a Libra Five, you have a timeless charm. It makes you seem like an icon. You captivate and are ready for fun. Your lively and spontaneous nature makes you the life of the party, as if you're always in a personal fantasy world. Yet, you're quick to flee from anything that feels restrictive.

All things sensual fascinate you. You have likely explored every aspect of it with great interest. Some may misinterpret your charm as romantic interest. So, be mindful of how you come across. You enjoy dating and exploring options. But, you tend to settle on one person who captures your interest.

You excel in glamorous fields like film, fashion, art, music, and public relations. Your talent for promotion and creativity makes you stand out. This is true whether you work in high-end clubs, manage boutiques, or hold flashy roles. You dislike routine. You thrive in jobs that involve teaching, investigation, or psychoanalysis.

You are a master of style and taste, known for your charm and sharp wit. Your taste in beauty and fashion makes you a key figure in social circles. Your instincts help you spot the right trends and people. You are an invaluable guide in both high-end and trendy places.

Libra 6: The Imaginative Storyteller

Peaceful, Unselfish, Manipulative, Self-righteous, Resolute, Artistic, Procrastinating, Susceptible to Flattery, Altruistic, Loving, Self-absorbed, Cooperative, Responsible, Domineering

As a Libra Six, you embody a mix of idealism and creativity, striving for peace and justice in every aspect of life. Your self-righteousness or manipulation might annoy some. But, your dedication to your causes and loved ones inspires many.

In relationships, people know you for your deep affection and expressiveness. You shower your partner with compliments and affection. However, your high ideals and standards may present challenges in maintaining long-term relationships. It's vital to have a partner who returns your love and respect. It's tough when they don't meet your expectations or appreciate your efforts. Don't use relationships to try to "fix" or change someone.

Your strong beliefs and ability to inspire others suit you for leadership, diplomacy, or teaching. You excel in roles like ambassador or motivational speaker. They should let you advocate for important causes and be a good example. Your job may be a paradox. It uses your talents for one goal, while seeking peace and goodwill for another.

Love and recognition fuel your motivation, and your ability to pick up on emotional subtleties is a valuable asset. Stay away from the temptation to play the martyr or tally up your acts of giving versus receiving. Use your gift of sensing and sharing messages of harmony. Balance your high ideals with practical methods. This will make your efforts rewarding and valued.

Libra 7: The Eloquent Dreamer

Articulate, logical, arrogant, distant, warm, selective, adaptable, distrustful, educated, cultured, concealed, sophisticated, and progressive

Being a Libra Seven, you love the refined and intellectual. Yet, you yearn for connection and perfection. You approach life with sophistication and a cerebral, personalised touch. You cherish the idea of soulmates and perfect harmony. Yet, you consistently face challenges in reconciling your dreams with real, meaningful relationships.

You seek a partner who meets your high standards. If they seem stronger in both body and mind,. Share your refined tastes and deep fantasies. You crave a relationship that transcends the ordinary, exploring transcendent, mystical experiences. You have high standards and a rich fantasy life. But this can cause disillusionment when real-world relationships fall short of your ideals. Your love life is a mix of passion and reflection. You seek a deep, spiritual connection, not just physicality.

Your career must resonate with your soul. You find fulfilment in the artistic fields. Your ability to evoke deep emotions makes you successful in roles that allow for self-expression and creativity. Whether you're performing, writing, or curating, you aim to touch hearts and minds. You also like the sciences and social work. They should let you use your analytical skills to help others. You seek to express your vision and to affect others through your work.

You have a unique talent for inspiring others to dream and believe in possibilities. Your unwavering faith in a better world and your passion for idealism are infectious, encouraging those around you to strive for more. Your quest for perfection may feel elusive. But, your idealism inspires others. It gives them hope and motivation. Keep nurturing your dreams. Use your gifts to inspire change. Explore the potential within yourself and others.

Libra 8: The Justice-Driven Visionary

Fair-minded, Realistic, Acquisitive, Aggressive, Philosophical, Authoritative, Extravagant, Workaholic, Courteous, Accomplished, Exploitative, Materialistic, Equable, Understanding

You, as a Libra Eight,, combine principled idealism with practical determination. A profound commitment to upholding justice and fairness, as well as an insatiable desire for personal and professional accomplishment, defines your approach to life. Your ability to analyse situations and confront obstacles shows a remarkable blend of strategic intuition and ethical determination.

Love ignites a fiery passion within you, driving you to extraordinary lengths to express it. Your romantic nature, connected to your values, makes you desire a partner who shares your intensity and dedication. Your preference is for exclusive relationships, but you can be open to transparent arrangements if required. In your perspective, marriage is a long-term commitment that should cause mutual benefit and satisfaction. You combine possessiveness with a sincere wish for partnership and personal development.

Curiosity characterises your professional journey and drive. At the start, it's common to change jobs while trying to discover your true vocation. Once you know your objectives, you chase them with unwavering resolve. Success, recognition, and financial stability motivate you. Roles that require public influence and strategic decision-making are where you thrive, and you always stay aware of your work environment. If a job falls short of your expectations, you are unafraid to pursue more satisfying opportunities, which highlights the curiosity that characterises your professional journey.

Embrace your role as a revolutionary philosopher and unleash your potential as a guiding force for positive change. You possess a captivating ability to advocate for justice and progress because of your blend of tolerance, intellect, and persuasive skills. Your steadfast dedication to your beliefs and your capacity to motivate others can create meaningful change in society. Your determination can turn ideas into action and inspire others to join your mission for a better world.

Libra 9: The Visionary Humanitarian

Sophisticated, generous, superficial, indulgent, philanthropic, mystical, escapist, inconsiderate, cultured, imaginative, hesitant, exacting, peaceful, and appealing

Your Libra Nine nature combines a love for humanity with a creative touch. Motivated by an intense yearning for impact, you have a near-messianic compulsion to save the world or ignite inspiration in others. Your vision aims to uplift individuals through either creative expression or a strong dedication to social causes. You perceive yourself as a catalyst, capable of differing in both individuals and societies.

The way you love is a unique blend of mental connection and physical charm. You prioritise meaningful conversations and emotional connections over mere physical attraction. Under your polished and distant façade, you possess a deep capacity for tenderness and affection. While you may attract attention and admiration, your primary concerns lie in broader humanitarian matters rather than personal bonds. It doesn't imply a deficiency in your romantic skills.

The choices you make in your career show a desire to have an impact and inspire others. Ideal roles for you include those where you can be a public figure, creative force, or humanitarian advocate. Consider exploring public relations, media, or the performing arts for a sense of fulfilment. Your strengths are also well-suited for careers involving one-on-one interactions, such as psychology or alternative healing practices. Your talent for connecting with others and your ability to understand societal trends make you perfect for roles that involve shaping public perception or introducing new ideas.

The key to unlocking your greatest potential is to envision a better world and inspire others to pursue it. Striking a balance between idealistic dreams and practical realities can be challenging. Focus on building stronger and more rewarding connections, both personally and professionally. Your gift of imagination is a valuable advantage. By taking action, you can lead change and bring your ideal utopia closer to reality. Despite the obstacles, your determination to make a positive impact has the power to create a significant transformation in the world.

Scorpio 1: The Driven Innovator

Bold, Direct, Ambitious, Independent, Inventive, Skeptical, Impatient, Thoughtful, Tenacious, Selfish

As a Scorpio One, you approach life with intense focus and curiosity. Since you were young, your curiosity has led you to seek the hidden truths in everything, often surprising others with your insightful observations.

Your approach to love shows a perfect balance between passion and practicality. When someone captures your interest, you adapt to their distinctive qualities, building a strong and nurturing relationship. You prioritise family values and aim for a supportive and caring relationship.

Your constant drive for personal growth and change makes you stand out. You don't settle for shallow achievements. You motivate those around you to achieve their highest potential, as your desire for growth is contagious. Your intensity and determination make you both captivating and intimidating to others. Yet, behind this strong facade, there is a compassionate nature that aims to uplift and empower fellow travellers.

Financial success isn't your sole focus in your professional life. You prioritise stability at first, but your long-term aim is to find a career that fulfils you and matches your aspirations. Your drive and self-reliance enable you to attain both financial and personal triumphs.

Your natural talent lies in inspiring others through your innovative thinking and decisive actions. Through living and pursuing your genuine passions, you show others how to tap into their potential and accomplish their objectives.

Scorpio 2: The Gracious Executive

Energetic, Compassionate, Gracious, Indecisive, Supportive, Shy, Tenacious, Persuasive, Skeptical, Self-critical, Quick-witted, Nervous, Intense, Conscientious

Being a Scorpio Two means you have a thoughtful and calculated approach to life, always striving for the best outcome for everyone involved. Despite your ability to bounce back from errors, you aim to prevent letting others down. Your tendency to be private often results in you handling personal matters on your own, without seeking external help.

When starting romantic relationships, you might overlook subtle signs of affection, confusing them with simple friendliness. Genuine emotions lead to a deep appreciation for commitment and the significant bonds that accompany it. You believe that love and friendship build a fulfilling relationship. As a parent, you value each stage of your child's development and embrace changes in family dynamics with excitement and attentiveness.

Fields like law, medicine, and entertainment offer you the opportunity to pursue meaningful work that aligns with your values, given your professional interests. Alternative 2: Creative careers like writing or other artistic endeavours could be accessible to you through your talents. You aim for the goal of discovering a career that aligns with your desires and principles.

In both your home environment and how you interact with others, it is evident that you possess a refined and thoughtful nature. Balancing indecision and determination is difficult, but crucial for a fulfilling life.

Scorpio 3: The Enterprising Romantic

Constructive, Imaginative, Shrewd, Scattered, Curious, Quick, Impulsive, Verbose, Practical, Sociable, Aggressive, Extravagant, Enterprising, Expressive

Scorpio Threes are excellent communicators and problem solvers, finding creative solutions to everyday challenges. Your practical yet imaginative approach makes life easier for those around you, whether you're guiding a friend through or convincing them. You have a generous nature when sharing ideas, but you also believe in empowering others to find their own way.

Winning your heart demands more than mere charm. Winning your heart demands more than mere charm; it requires finding a partner who can match your energy and commitment in the long run, which is what matters. You desire a meaningful bond that surpasses surface-level attraction, prioritising a partnership founded on respect and common aspirations.

In your professional journey, you consider each job as a stepping stone towards bigger goals, like a dream vacation or a leadership role. Your skill at multitasking keeps you focused and ready to take advantage of new opportunities.

You have a unique ability to blend creativity and practicality, making your dreams a reality while staying grounded. By embracing love, friendship, and determination, you not only reach your goals, but also inspire those around you. To keep making progress, it's crucial to stay focused and not let distractions derail you.

The key aspects of your personality are your natural resilience and resourcefulness. You never give up when confronted with challenges. Your determination not only helps you overcome challenges, but also motivates others to do the same. Your natural charm attracts people, and your ability to stay composed under pressure makes you a dependable and influential presence in both personal and professional contexts. Prioritising self-reflection and personal growth will strengthen your leadership skills, allowing you to inspire others and make a lasting impact.

Scorpio 4: The Dynamic Master Builder

Courageous, Energetic, Executive, Ambitious, Practical, Determined, Logical, Good-hearted, Suspicious, Wilful, Blunt, Undemonstrative, Too Busy, Needs Proof

Being a Scorpio Four, your determination and persistence make you relentless in pursuing ideas. When you dedicate yourself to a project, others either support you or understand staying out of your way. With your unwavering determination and practical mindset, you can turn dreams into tangible achievements, overcoming any obstacles in your path.

Since you were young, you've been pursuing your ideal life. Despite valuing stability, you find yourself drawn to relationships that offer something extraordinary. Your ability to balance passion and practicality ensures that your life stays exciting, even when you have a lot on your plate.

Your work should be something you find enjoyable. You excel in roles that appreciate diligence and logical thinking, thriving in environments that emphasise transparency and straightforwardness. Your preference is clear communication and surrounding yourself with enthusiastic team members who share your dedication and vision.

Your determination to your ideas is profound, and you aim to bring others on board with you. However, it is crucial for you to prioritise maintaining a healthy work-life balance because of your intense drive. Keep the energy and enthusiasm alive to inspire those around you.

Your dynamic and knowledgeable nature inspires others, making you a valuable mentor and leader. By inspiring and guiding those around you, you enhance your team's strength and your own achievements. Embracing this role allows you to create a positive and lasting impact in your personal and professional life.

Scorpio 5: The Worldly Wanderer

Freedom-Loving, Blunt, Restless, Energetic, Impulsive, Fickle, Quick-Witted, Curious, Secretive, Hasty, Constructive, Resourceful

Since you were young, your wanderlust has fuelled your desire to explore the world as a Scorpio Five. Your insatiable craving for new experiences keeps your life vibrant and filled with excitement, even when things don't always go as planned. Whether venturing far or near, you are on the go, eager to discover the unfamiliar.

As you search for a partner, you hope to find someone who matches your enthusiasm for adventure and will join you on your life's journey. It's crucial for you to have a partner who can bring stability and excitement to equal measure. Your intention is to incorporate your family into your trips, using your escapades to teach them about the world. Valuing loyalty and expecting the same level of commitment from your partner is essential.

Your career is driven by a focus on meaningful work and measurable achievements, rather than financial worries. You have a natural inclination towards fields like travel, physical fitness, or expedition management, allowing you to engage in hands-on activities and connect with fascinating people. Instead of prioritising high salaries for financial security, you focus on personal satisfaction and finding joy in your work.

You build your reputation by being straightforward and perceptive, without sugarcoating the truth. Your astute observations and extensive experiences enable you to understand others. Yet, it's crucial to consider the impact of your straightforwardness on others. Balancing honesty and empathy is crucial for navigating social situations and fostering positive relationships.

Combining your adventurous personality and straightforward approach creates a captivating and influential presence. Embrace exploration while being conscious of your words, and you'll enhance your life and the lives of those you meet.

Scorpio 6: The Dazzling Collective

Daring, Responsible, Aggressive, Self-Sacrificing, Focused, Artistic, Secretive, Domineering, Practical, Nurturing, Critical, Jealous, Curious, Idealistic

Love is the primary focus of your life as a Scorpio Six, and you embrace it in various ways such as through friends, family, and colleagues. Your aim is more than just seeking love.

With a keen eye, you navigate your social circles, evaluating and updating your mental files on everyone. This approach helps you balance friendliness with a constant awareness of opportunities for growth and transformation.

In love, you have high expectations and are looking for a partner who can meet them. The initial thrill of a relationship may not last, but you place importance on lasting commitment and the profoundness of true love. You value fidelity and exploration. You also treasure being a parent and aim to be a lifelong friend to your children, giving them unconditional love and support.

Among the subjects that interest you are history, beauty, writing, and education. As an educator, theorist, or author, your wide range of interests can pave the way for a successful career.

Because of your motivation to educate and improve, you are effective in these areas. Finding a balance between personal and professional lives can be tough, but don't doubt your priorities. While financial stability is crucial, your major priority lies in creating a significant influence.

Your talent lies in motivating people to exceed their own expectations and reach their full potential. One of your greatest strengths is your ability to inspire and motivate others, and it brings you immense satisfaction to see them succeed. Keep in mind that your powerful personality could damage feelings or sever connections while defending your ideas or projects. Balancing assertiveness and empathy is key to successful relationships and goal attainment.

Scorpio 7: The Practical Perfectionist

Energetic, Perfectionist, Skeptical, Secretive, Compassionate, Intellectual, Self-Critical, Argumentative, Tenacious, Analytical, Intense, Suspicious, Quick-Witted, Private

Your curiosity about Earth's rotation and gravity, as a Scorpio Seven, foreshadowed your lifelong quest for knowledge. Your motivation originates from a need to uncover and grasp unfamiliar subjects, striving for unconventional achievements. You may strive for awards or engaging in unique pursuits because of your competitive nature and desire for recognition.

When you're in a relationship, your passion intensifies despite being hidden. Before getting into romance, you prioritise honesty and clarity. Delaying marriage is possible if you come across a partner who aligns with your intellect and emotions, as you'll be ready to commit. You find joy in the enigma of relationships and a desire to navigate life's intricacies alongside your partner.

Your strengths lie in roles that demand both intellect and intuition. Your ability to solve mysteries and charisma assists you in handling intricate scenarios. Recognition is important to you, and you manage money by adapting to diverse financial situations. In the realms of leadership, innovation, or business operations, we gain insights from our experiences and apply them to future endeavours.

Get a head start by developing skills that will lead to your success. Your thirst for knowledge leads you to uncover valuable understandings. Take a moment to reflect on the irreversible consequences before making any major decisions. Achieve success by balancing your intense drive with thoughtful consideration.

Scorpio 8: The Stylish Traveler

Patient, Authoritative, Suspicious, Workaholic, Determined, Global View, Inconsistent, Impersonal, Constructive, Enduring, Ambitious, Indecisive, Quick-Witted, Capable

Being a Scorpio Eight, your life is far from simple; it is intricate and multi-faceted, like a diamond. Recognise that individuals and circumstances are intricate, understanding that each person possesses a unique combination of strengths and weaknesses. By taking on challenges, you show your understanding that life is complex.

During your travels, you could form a meaningful connection with a partner by bonding over shared stories and experiences. When you begin your relationships, excitement and adventure marks them, but as time goes on, they become more stable with aligned goals. You imagine a future that harmonises practicality and romance, integrating individual spaces and shared aspirations to nurture your bond.

Respect and financial rewards are essential in your life. Roles those provides recognition and a fair return for your efforts, like reporting, education, or executive positions, are where you excel. Whether you're performing or leading, you excel when others acknowledge and reward your contributions. Despite the ebb and flow of money, your primary motivation lies in making impactful contributions.

Since a young age, you've had ambitious dreams, like owning Disneyland. Your high standards and relentless work ethic inspire those around you as you strive to achieve your goals. Remember to find a balance and cherish moments of relaxation and togetherness with loved ones. True fulfilment requires both support and downtime, even for the most driven individuals.

Combining your aptitude for managing complexity and your relentless pursuit of success and recognition makes you a force to be reckoned with. Achieve a fulfilling and well-rounded life by balancing ambitious goals and moments of relaxation and connection.

Scorpio 9: The Mystic Manager

Practical, Compassionate, Forceful, Detached, Energetic, Impartial, Moody, Careless, Tenacious, Charismatic, Ambitious, Needs Approval, Smart, Performer

From a young age, as a Scorpio Nine, you had a strong connection to the mystical and intangible, finding comfort in imaginary companions and contemplating ideas like reincarnation. Your lifelong connection to the unseen realm has shaped you, combining practical wisdom with deep insights into existence.

You balance casual charm with an unwavering pursuit of perfection in your relationships. The way you love is both generous and creative, as you share your deepest vulnerabilities with the people you care about. Despite the occasional distance, your love remains unwavering and devoted.

Your innate magnetism and dynamic vitality make you stand out in any professional domain. Leading a team or working, you excel and attract support. Your career options are wide-ranging, including writing and architecture, and your empathy and distinct understanding of individuals will contribute to your achievements.

You have the power to decide between fame and infamy, and your actions will always attract attention. The way you can create deep connections and identify past-life links makes each interaction unforgettable. Relationships may change, but each one leaves a lasting impact, reflecting prizing your individual journey.

Embrace your individual journey, recognising that your influence is both important and everlasting. Your unique combination of mystical insight, charismatic presence, and deep connections guarantees a lasting and unforgettable impact on the world.

Sagittarius 1: The Fearless Philosopher

Energetic, Inventive, Impulsive, Headstrong, Enthusiastic, Original, Fanatical, Iconoclastic, Open-minded, Self-starter, Blunt, Overbearing, Fun-loving, Daring

As a young Sagittarius One, your fascination with maps and global capitals fuelled an unquenchable thirst for adventure and diverse cultures. Your life resembles an open road, where unexpected twists and exhilarating findings await, reflecting your deep curiosity and love for discovering new things.

Independence is a fundamental principle for you, and you value mutual devotion, loyalty, and shared passions in your relationships. Your perfect partnership includes going on adventures, having deep discussions, and staying curious. Commitment, for you, involves sharing life's journey with someone who respects and supports your need for freedom, rather than placing limitations.

Your aspirations are far from ordinary. Your dedication to achieving goals drives your passion for career changes and new ventures. Despite prioritising ideals over personal relationships, your energy and enthusiasm ensure success in various roles, such as an athlete, business leader, or comedian. If you desire a career that allows you the freedom to adapt and unleash your creativity, always spearheading your own ventures, then...

Your ability to combine humour and idealism enables you to create a distinct positive influence on the world. As a skilled creator, you are crafting new visions and putting in endless effort to bring them to fruition. Like classic Disney songs such as "When You Wish Upon a Star" and "Whistle While You Work," you derive joy from connecting and inspiring others through your endeavours.

Let your adventurous spirit and innovative mindset guide you as you make a meaningful impact on the world. By staying devoted to your passions and motivating others, your journey becomes meaningful and influential.

Sagittarius 2: The Mellow Maestro

Striving, Supportive, Thin-skinned, Extremist, Tolerant, Charming, Undisciplined, Nervous, Imaginative, Intuitive, Brash, Procrastinating, Innovative, Sincere

With your Sagittarius Two sign, you have a poetic nature and a romantic spirit, driven by a vivid imagination and an optimistic view of what lies ahead. Despite your modesty in displaying your talents, like playing Chopin or creating art, the depth of your hidden skills takes aback your close friends. Your creative mindset enables you to overcome life's obstacles.

You value commitment. You want a partner who uplifts your self-worth and values your uniqueness while also embracing your aspirations. In love, you prioritise emotional and intellectual compatibility and are both passionate and experimental before committing. Your nurturing nature ensures that your relationships remain steady and meaningful.

Careers in the arts, like artist, actor, healer, mystic, or writer, are a great fit for you with your vivid imagination. Your unique blend of creativity, empathy, and ambition positions you to thrive as a leader in any area of interest. You have a standout quality that makes you shine in painting, writing, or directing.

You add a poetic touch to life with your distinctive charm and style. Inspire others to discover and embrace their artistic sides by conquering your shyness. Your determination and firm beliefs are apparent as you pursue your convictions, revealing your true potential as a leader and creative force.

Welcome your artistic inclinations and allow your imaginative spirit to guide you in realising your capabilities. By combining creativity and leadership, you make a lasting impression on those around you without compromising yourself.

Sagittarius 3: The Winsome Wanderer

Cheerful, Expressive, Impractical, Flighty, Optimistic, Creative, Fickle, Profligate, Clever, Merry, Gabby, Unstable, Idealistic, Inspirational

A Sagittarius Three, you exude a magical charm driven by your ideals and passions. Like Tinker-bell, you exude enthusiasm and connect with kindred spirits, engaging strangers with your lively and curious personality. Your constant inquiries and genuine truthfulness may surprise people, but your motives are always good and sincere.

Experiencing love is like embarking on an exhilarating journey, filled with the awe and excitement of a child. Regardless of how a relationship ends, you remain hopeful. Despite facing obstacles, your heart remains strong and unwavering, embracing love with enthusiasm.

You bring limitless energy and excitement to new projects, even if finishing them can be difficult for you. The perfect job for you would involve flexibility, such as working in public relations or marketing, managing events, and interacting with new people outside the usual 9-to-5 routine.

Your exuberant passion for life is one of your greatest assets. Maintaining a balance between enthusiasm and practical action is crucial to avoid overcommitment or breaking promises. By harnessing your energy, you have the power to motivate and rally others to back your causes, creating a significant influence in any endeavour you pursue.

Harness your innate charm and lively nature to inspire and drive others. When you combine enthusiasm and follow-through, you can make your dreams a reality and succeed in all your endeavours.

Sagittarius 4: The Audacious Auditor

Honest, Hearty, Inconsistent, Overworked, Humorous, Nature-loving, Self-absorbed, Contrary, Honourable, Methodical, Hotheaded, Undemonstrative, Zesty, Persevering

Sagittarius Four, You navigate life with a quest for balance between feeling grounded and resisting the mundane. A hard worker by nature, you can find beauty in the everyday grind, despite occasional grumbling. This pursuit of the ideal extends to your personal life, where you often balance restoring your home and indulging in hobbies with a touch of humor and zest.

Romance is a balancing act for you. You desire stability but also crave freedom, often finding yourself in relationships that reflect this push and pull. Your efforts to make things work are sincere, but if a relationship falters, you move on quickly and without significant emotional scars. Your busy life and various commitments can sometimes serve as a shield against deeper connections.

You excel in roles that challenge you both mentally and physically, from technical positions like sports car or computer technician to careers involving planning and engineering. Your skill in evaluating situations makes you a strong candidate for financial planning or CPA roles. Your quick wit and charm also lend themselves to the arts, where your distinctive presence can shine, whether on stage or in writing.

Your resilience and practicality serve as an inspiration to others. With laughter and tenacity, you tackle hardships head-on. Under strain, your spirit soars, inspiring those around you to rise above adversity. Your positivity and reliability make you a cherished friend. You are a role model for handling tough times with grace and resilience.

Sagittarius 5: The Merry Navigator

Spontaneous, Adventurous, Reckless, Restless, Outgoing, Communicative, Fickle, Tactless

As a Sagittarius Five, you are always on a quest for fresh adventures and experiences in life. Your eagerness to explore, experiment, and embark on thrilling journeys introduces you to diverse individuals and cultures. Your thrill comes from the journey, not the destination, transforming each moment into a discovery.

In a romantic relationship, you seek a partner who shares your love for adventure and can keep up with your lively rhythm. Long-term commitments can be challenging for you because of your thriving excitement and spontaneity. You want someone who has the same zest for life and can embrace the unpredictability that comes with your spontaneous nature.

You thrive in careers that involve mobility and new experiences. Whether you're a flight attendant, pilot, journalist, or travel guide, you thrive in adventurous and dynamic environments. You have a strong passion for standing up for what's right, making a career in justice advocacy a perfect fit for you.

Balancing your adventurous spirit with responsibility is crucial for unlocking your full potential. Although being spontaneous is a strength of yours, developing the ability to commit and follow through can enhance relationships and long-term achievements. Find equilibrium and savour the best of both worlds—exciting escapades and meaningful, enduring connections.

Nurture your innate curiosity and longing for discovery while staying grounded in your responsibility to build a fulfilling and thrilling life. This approach empowers you to navigate your journey and maximise every opportunity.

Sagittarius 6: The Electric Educator

Supportive, Idealistic, Outspoken, Reckless, Joyous, Warm

A unique combination of idealism and duty characterises you as a Sagittarius Six. Your unwavering dedication to your principles compels you to adopt resolute positions on significant matters, and while you're not extreme, your eagerness guides you towards unanticipated courses. By adopting this idealistic approach, your life gains a profound philosophical dimension, shaping you into a person who is both contemplative and vocal.

In your personal life, you're devoted and accountable, always thinking ahead. The thought of family life fills you with excitement, and you approach it with joy and a sense of thrill. As a parent, you celebrate not only the achievements but also the funny and lighthearted moments that come with them. One of your greatest joys is sharing adventures with loved ones, and your caring nature makes your family feel loved and uplifted.

You excel in roles where you can assist others. In social work, healthcare, or teaching, your humanitarian instincts inspire you to create a tangible impact in the lives of others. With your commitment and idealism, you can assume leadership roles in the ministry or military, as your effective management of people serves as inspiration to those around you.

The joy you bring to those around you results from your delightful and clever nature. Your positive outlook and captivating personal stories attract people and earn their trust. The way you share your experiences and your optimistic outlook have a natural ability to inspire others. Despite this, it is important to stay open-minded and avoid getting too stuck in your ways. To balance your beliefs with others' views, embrace new ideas and agree to disagree.

As a Sagittarius Six, your idealism, sense of duty, and warm personality make you a source of support and joy for others. When you balance your firm beliefs with remaining open, you can continue to inspire and uplift those around you without compromising your values.

Sagittarius 7: The Animated Analyst

Original, Truth-seeking, Absentminded, Knowledgeable, Curious, Mystical

As a Sagittarius Seven, you seek understanding. You are an innovator with a mix of optimism and cynicism. You believe that with the right combination of research and a bit of luck, things will work out as they should. A strong sense of destiny guides you. It draws you to explore deep ideas, like fate and the mysteries of life.

Your high ideals can be impractical, especially in love. In your youth, you might mistake flings for true love. But, as you mature, you learn to value commitment. You learn settling down doesn't mean losing your freedom. It enhances your relationships. You can now share your journey with someone who respects your need to explore and grow.

In your career, you excel in jobs that test your mind and creativity. You excel in teaching, research, and writing. You thrive in roles that let you explore complex ideas and create unique insights. Your ability to stay creative makes you a standout in fields like academia or satire. They value innovative thinking and a sharp mind. You need a job that keeps you stimulated and allows you to learn and grow.

Your sharp mind and strong ideals could affect the world. However, it's important to remember that people are not platforms for your ideas. By balancing your fiery spirit with kindness, you'll connect with others. You'll inspire them with your ideas, but also with your warmth.

As a Sagittarius Seven, you must balance seeking knowledge with human connection. By combining your ideas with compassion, you'll achieve your goals. You'll also bring others with you. This will make your impact both meaningful and lasting.

Sagittarius 8: The Steadfast Strategist

Honourable, Ambitious, Workaholic, Frank, Dynamic, Capable

As a Sagittarius Eight, people know you for your drive and your fast-paced life. You juggle high-stakes business deals and social causes. Your energy seems boundless. This drive makes you a force in any field. But you might feel detached. Your packed schedule leaves little time for downtime.

In love, you're not one for traditional dating. You're so focused on your goals that relationships take a backseat. They only fit into your life when they don't disrupt your flow. If romance enters your busy life, you'll treat it like a business deal. You'll negotiate time and space to make it work. Your ideal partner can match your fast-paced, flexible, and travel-loving lifestyle. They must see relationships as more about logistics than limitations.

Your exceptional abilities are highlighted in intense situations, and you always rise to the occasion. CEO, politician, or analyst are positions that suit you well. Leadership attracts you, and you relish the challenge of advancing in the corporate world. Your drive for success can make you restless, always seeking the next enormous opportunity. Your drive is admirable. But quick gains can be fleeting. Careful, long-term planning is key to sustaining your success.

Your unique potential lies in your ability to blend capitalism with social responsibility. You can make a big impact by aligning your goals with causes that matter to you. Balance your drive for success with a touch of realism. Choose your battles. This will direct your energy toward meaningful efforts that leave a lasting legacy.

As a Sagittarius Eight, your journey is to find balance. It combines ambition with connections. The focus is on quick gains and lasting success. The key is your drive and desired impact. By channeling your energy into causes you're passionate about, you can have unlimited impact..

Sagittarius 9: The Artistic Adventurer

Compassionate, Creative, Broad-minded, Egotistical, Unrealistic

As a Sagittarius Nine, you are a mix of deep thought and high ideals. You often become a moral crusader, with a flair for dramatic, noble gestures. Your compassion and creativity make you captivating. You blend deep ideas with entertaining, thought-provoking stories. People like your knack for discussing serious topics with a light touch. It makes complex ideas more engaging and easier to grasp.

In relationships, you often play the role of the rescuer. You want to help those in tough situations. Your desire to save them comes from a sense of nobility. Your intentions are sincere. But be mindful of the balance. Help others, but don't get too involved in their problems. Your urge to rescue others can stem from your own needs. So make sure you base your relationships on mutual support rather than one-sided help.

In the corporate world, your personality and charisma are your greatest assets. You excel in jobs that allow for creativity and travel. They let your storytelling and unique views shine. As a news correspondent, diplomat, tour operator, and artist, you captivate audiences. You leave a lasting impression. You have refined tastes. They encourage you to collect fine art and luxury items. They reflect your love of beauty and craftsmanship.

Your charm and understanding of people give you an edge in all relationships. You can inspire and lead others. You do this by sharing your unique path with enthusiasm and conviction. But, it's important to be open-minded. This is true, especially when meeting people or ideas that differ from your own. Sometimes, the best learning and connections come from those who challenge your views.

As a Sagittarius Nine, you must balance your high ideals with life's practicalities. Embrace your role as a moral crusader, but do so with an awareness of your own needs and boundaries. Stay open to new experiences. Keep your compassion. You can grow and inspire those around you.

Capricorn 1: The Tenacious Trailblazer

Diplomatic, Inventive, Reliable, Stubborn, Domineering, Courageous

As a Capricorn One, you shine in the spotlight. It's not that you seek attention. Your drive and determination set you apart from the crowd. Your dedication to pursuing goals or high standards makes you stand out.

In relationships, you value both attractiveness and substance in a partner. You might be attracted to someone who catches everyone's attention. But you want a deep connection. You want a partner who supports your ambitions. Family is central to your life. You connect more with your kids as they grow older. Still, you see them as vital to your journey. In marriage, you are not one to rush in–you check on your partner, ensuring they align with your values and long-term goals. You expect a relationship filled with mutual respect and passion.

Financial stability is a significant focus for you. You believe in working hard and are meticulous about managing your finances, tracking every penny to ensure you're on the right path. You prefer to invest in things that are built to last and meet your high standards, choosing quality over quantity in your approach to money. This mindset shows in your career choices. As a designer, engineer, or manager, you seek roles that bring both satisfaction and success. Respect and expertise are highly valued in your work. Your ambition is to attain promotions and better opportunities.

Your clear vision for improvement extends to both large scale and immediate environments. Your logic in ideas and talent for turning plans into reality attract people to you. However, it's essential for you to remember prizing balancing work with relaxation. Self-care boosts your productivity. It also helps you lead and succeed long term.

Your discipline and focus on long-term goals make you a natural leader. Others look to you for guidance and inspiration. By maintaining a balance between your ambitions and your well-being, you can continue to excel and inspire those around you.

Capricorn 2: The Aspiring Ambassador

Ambitious, Tactful, Dependable, Timid, Supportive, Moody

As a Capricorn Two, you excel at juggling many roles. You guide people through a maze of tasks and priorities. Your leadership style is a mix of charm and discretion. It lets you navigate complex agendas while delegating tasks to others. This ability to manage and organise is one of your strongest assets.

A romantic heart lies beneath your tough and composed exterior. You want a partner who can understand your world. They must be strong enough to break through your emotional walls. You are drawn to someone who has both intelligence and courage. They must handle life's logic, like spreadsheets, and your guarded emotions. You hope the right person is out there for you. This is despite past flings and failed near-engagements.

In your career, your sharp intuition and meticulous research set you apart. You want financial success. But you also seek recognition and validation in your field. You may explore many career paths. Balance traditional roles with creative pursuits. You strive to be the best at whatever you choose. Your skill in predicting trends and outcomes is valuable. You use research and intuition to do it. Those close to you especially value your practical vision.

You know it's vital to keep close ties with friends and family, even as you chase your goals. Your pay-check and career matter. But you value your personal connections that ground you. Due to your practical insights and foresight, you have earned a trusted advisory status. The way you maintain your work-life balance reflects your disciplined approach to living.

Thanks to your unique combination of practicality, intuition, and emotion, you excel in life. It also helps you keep strong, meaningful relationships. By staying true to your values, you can find a balance. Nurture your work and personal life to find fulfilment.

Capricorn 3: The Imaginative Manager

Sensible, Creative, Conventional, Sociable, Nervous, Imaginative, Brooding

As a Capricorn Three, you blend practicality and creativity. It helps you navigate life with realism and imagination. You may have grown up with dreams and a touch of whimsy. But you've learned to ground those dreams in reality. You now use a pragmatic approach to turn your aspirations into achievements. Your charisma and energy keep you youthful. You stay engaged and eager for life well into old age.

In love, you embrace its many forms with a dynamic and adventurous spirit. You know that love can be lasting and committed. But you also value the beauty of brief passions and connections. You have a fluid, open view of romance. You want to experience all its facets. Not every relationship will last a lifetime. But you value the moments and bonds you create. Each experience helps you grow.

In your career, your work ethic and creativity drive success. You turn bold ideas into reality. You excel at managing your money. It helps you meet your goals and avoid overspending. Your imagination often leads to unique opportunities. Your vast network of friends helps. By embracing both the practical and the aspirational, you can blend hard work with a touch of luck. This can lead to a fulfilling and successful life.

Your Capricorn's practicality and a Three's creativity will bring you outstanding success. With focus and direction, you can excel in your work and personal life. Your resilience and creativity drive your success. They also inspire those around you. By balancing your grounded approach with your imagination, you'll find your greatest strength. It's in merging these two sides.

Capricorn 4: The Persevering Perfectionist

Aspiring, Persistent, Conceited, Competent, Nervous, Practical, Stubborn

As a Capricorn Four, you excel at creating something from nothing. Your block-building childhood and current achievements prove it. Your patience and drive let you start small and then grow. You learn from the best to ensure your success. If others underestimate you, your persistence will impress.

Your approach to relationships is a blend of substance and sensuality. A partner with high standards is something you value. You hope to find someone who matches your intellect and wit, both in and out of the bedroom. Many times, people marry early in hopes of a long-lasting commitment. But you are ready to seek another partner if needed. Your responsibilities extend to being a devoted parent, adding joy and a touch of whimsy to your life.

Practical experience and cautious decision-making shape your career path. You are adept at learning from mistakes without taking undue risks. In your work, you thrive on involvement and hands-on management. You prefer to work with a capable team to execute projects. Your strengths are in fields that need detailed planning. These include accounting, engineering, and construction.

Your optimism and hard work give you a backup plan. You often prove doubters wrong by overcoming challenges. You are a dedicated friend and ally. But, you must balance work and personal life. Make time to relax and expand your social circle.

You cannot excel in every area at once without support from others.

Capricorn 5: The Reliable Risk-Taker

Conscientious, Versatile, Cautious, Reckless, Down-to-earth, Curious, Economical, Adventurous, Restless, Generous, Resourceful

You Capricorn Five know how to balance adventure and routine. So, make time for fun in your busy schedule. You fit a variety of activities into your life. They include beach days, a bowling league, and family events. Your adventurous spirit shows in your hobbies and your approach to challenges. You live life to the fullest, but you stay organised.

You prefer people who share your interests and can keep up with your dynamic lifestyle. Physical attraction matters. But, you also want a partner who shares your intellect and sense of adventure. Despite having had some wild adventures, you now desire to settle down. You hope to find a partner for spontaneous adventures and a strong, conventional family life. A partner who can keep up with both the thrill and the responsibilities of life is important to you.

Your concern lies in financial security. It lets you enjoy luxuries, like fine wines and ski trips. You work hard and spend. This lets you enjoy life while managing your money. You thrive in careers that are varied and challenging. They include machinery, manufacturing, entertainment, law, and journalism. Your curiosity and ideas make you a valuable asset. They hold value in any field that values exploration and new views.

The way you combine practicality with adventure makes you an intriguing figure. Your unique approach to balancing responsibility with excitement draws people in. From your enthusiasm and charisma comes your ability to inspire others. But you must weigh risks and consider the impact of your actions on those who follow you. Your energy and curiosity are great. But be cautious. It will keep you well and help you make a positive impact.

Capricorn 6: The Ambitious Idealist

Industrious, Nurturer, Suspicious, Self-righteous, Realistic, Loyal, Domineering, Moody, Fearless, Idealistic, Critical, Self-sacrificing, Resolute, Responsible

You are a Capricorn Six. The blending of ambition and idealism is evident in you. Nurturing others comes naturally to you, as you strive for high standards. Your drive is powerful. It comes with a sense of duty. But, it makes you critical or self-righteous. Like a modern-day Joan of Arc, you might have grand aspirations and a sense of destiny that guides your path.

A blend of idealism and practicality characterises your approach to relationships. A partner with high emotional, intellectual, and physical standards is what you are looking for. Finding the right match may involve dating multiple people. However, you want a deep and lasting connection with someone.

Your ideal partner shares your values and matches your ambitions.

Loyalty and dedication are central to your career approach. Colleagues are expected and inspired to show commitment. It is common for you to bring trusted associates along when you change jobs. You thrive in environments that value your efforts and allow your vision to flourish. If a job is dull or the workplace toxic, you seek new opportunities to shine.

Your natural inclination to guide and nurture others is both a strength and a potential pitfall. You believe your goals are right. You sometimes justify bad methods if they work. Your support is invaluable to those around you. But, don't let your dedication to others overshadow your own goals and well-being. Balancing your ideals with practicalities will help you succeed. It will bring you personal fulfilment and professional success.

Capricorn 7: The Selective Specialist

Generous, Intellectual, Reserved, Shrewd, Reliable, Articulate, Workaholic, Suspicious, Organised, Analytical, Cautious, Aloof, Persistent, Seeks Solitude

You a Capricorn Seven. You possess a profound and insightful disposition. Behind a calm and composed exterior, you often conceal it. Mixing your curiosity and secretive tendencies make you quite mysterious. It adds complexity and fascination to your character. Similar to the Capricorn Seven, you possess analytical and reserved qualities. You enjoy being alone and engaging in profound introspection.

In relationships, you value independence and the need for personal space. The partner you desire is someone who possesses sensitivity, attractiveness, and intelligence. Yet, they must acknowledge your need for personal space. In friends and partners, you select them with great care, treating them like family. Parenthood might not be your major focus. If you make the choice to be a parent, you must embrace it with dedication and responsibility. The perfect relationship balances closeness and freedom. Both partners flourishes with it.

You value financial privacy and handle your finances. You earn a noteworthy income, contribute, and sustain financial autonomy. Your work history exemplifies a strong work ethic and an unwavering commitment to being outstanding. However, it's possible for you to reject promotions that clash with your personal interests or side projects. Your analytical thinking and selective approach to work will lead to your success. You are skilled in both traditional professions and non-traditional endeavours.

Your pursuit of excellence and mastery surpasses expectations. It establishes you as an expert in your industry. Others find it both captivating and unsettling how you can simplify complex issues. Allow yourself to explore your mystical interests and enhance your psychic abilities. Still, ensure that you have time for yourself to grow and reflect. Cherish and cultivate your important connections, and prevent secrets from sabotaging future joy. When you share your knowledge and experiences, you motivate others to pursue their dreams and succeed. The point you're making is clear: if greatness is attainable for some, it is for others as well.

Capricorn 8: The Practical Philosopher

Impersonal, Realistic, Ambitious, Pretentious, Workaholic, Fearless, Capable, Critical, Materialistic, Resolute, Arbitrator

As a Capricorn Eight, you appear practical. There's a philosophical side to you as well. In your career and in life, you make calculated risks. Your aspiration is to achieve remarkable success through leadership. Making an impact and excelling is something you crave. In places where your ambition and organisational skills can shine, you thrive.

In relationships, you focus on personal happiness and will not settle for less. You weigh decisions like marriage. But when you set your heart on something, you follow it. You do so even if it defies logic. Your partner must support your pursuits. They must also understand your need to balance your goals with home life. Your unique charm adds a quirky touch to your relationships. Your approach to love is practical. Making sure that both passion and practicality are present is your responsibility.

Your strong work ethic and clear career vision guarantee your success. Being a planner and leader, you are adept at seeing things from a broad perspective. You assign regular chores. Your goal is to become well-off. You want for comfort and wealth. Your compassion shines through as you selflessly use your riches to help others. In recessions, you may run into financial difficulties. However, your work ethic and will to succeed are steadfast. It's crucial to keep in mind to balance work, play, and self-care.

Your belief in your ability to achieve and improve is a key asset. Whether you become a top executive or a performer, you inspire others through your actions and contributions. Your down-to-earth nature and generosity make you a role model, even if you don't seek the spotlight. With your capacity for tactile enjoyment and a full life, be mindful of your energy and health. Embrace your role as a guide and example, but also remember to take your own advice and practice self-care. Your potential lies in balancing your high aspirations with a grounded and enjoyable life.

Capricorn 9: The Deliberate Showman

Persistent, Generous, Brooding, Impersonal, Conscientious, Compassionate, Critical, Self-interested, Ambitious, Performer, Nervous, Inconsistent, Pragmatic, Charismatic

Capricorn Nines exhibit a blend of performance flair and persistent drive. You thrive on stage and in the limelight. You push your limits to captivate your audience. Like the famous Capricorn Nine, such as Paul Revere, Albert Schweitzer, and Elvis

Presley, you can turn your ambitions into reality. You do this through hard work and innovation.

In relationships, trust is something you prefer to build. You respond to physical attraction. But a committed relationship takes a more cautious approach. You seek a partner who not only understands and believes in you but also matches your intellectual and emotional needs. Your view of intimacy is performance-based. It mixes thoughtfulness with some kinkiness. Your ideal match is someone who can indulge in seductive games. They should share your passion for your career and the intricacies of life.

Your financial habits reflect a blend of extravagance and thriftiness. You can earn a lot. But you often worry about your finances. A good money management system or financial software could help. Managing finances or leading a team is where you excel. Roles with prime responsibility and visibility are where you thrive. If you enjoy engaging with a crowd or managing others, you prefer certain environments.

Despite your self-confidence, you may need boosts before big events. It might feel unusual to ask for help, but others are often eager to support you. With a constant influx of new ideas, focus can be tough. But your ability to turn these ideas into results is remarkable. You might not see yourself as a visionary, but your accomplishments and ability to bring your ideas to life often lead others to view you as such. We admire your talent for turning ideas into reality. It shows your unique blend of creativity and practical achievement.

Aquarius 1: The Pragmatic Pioneer

Leader, Bold, Extreme, Driven, Independent, Direct, Generous, Decisive, Aloof, Innovative

Since you were young, your Aquarius One personality has shown a strong desire for control and independence. Your drive to learn quickly and embrace new ideas motivates you to explore cutting-edge concepts, although it can be hard to stay consistent in completing tasks. The way you think ahead and embrace unexplored areas characterises your approach to both personal and professional undertakings.

In relationships, you place importance on having open and dynamic conversations, seeking direct interactions and honesty. You delay or approach commitment due to your need for independence and privacy, despite cherishing family and connections. Your preference is to balance personal freedom and nurturing relationships.

You thrive in professional roles that offer independence and acknowledgment. Dynamic environments are where your self-driven approach and innovative solutions can shine. Leadership positions are a perfect fit for you, as you enjoy leading instead of following, using your distinct perspective and creativity to advance.

Your remarkable memory and forward-thinking nature are important strengths. To unlock your full potential, find a balance between independence and supportive connections. Achieving a fulfilling life involves both relationships and personal freedom.

Aquarius 2: The Reserved Aristocrat

Determined, Persuasive, Secretive, Moody, Cooperative, Patient, Radical, Shy, Generous, Supportive, Quarrelsome, Worrisome, Eloquent, Gregarious

As an Aquarius Two, you've often felt out of sync with others, navigating life with a unique perspective that sets you apart. Shyness and indecision may hold you back. But, your sharp mind and innovative spirit can turn ideas into successful ventures.To unlock your potential, you must brace against the norm. The box is essential for this.

In relationships, you value both independence and companionship. You seek a partner who can share in your adventures and engage in deep, meaningful conversations. A successful relationship, for you, balances freedom with intimacy. You'd end a relationship if it threatened your independence. So, it's vital to find a partner who respects this need.

You're driven to contribute meaningful work and express your creativity. You excel in roles that offer the freedom to innovate and the opportunity for recognition. A strong network and peer recognition can boost your career. They can improve your performance and job satisfaction.

Your diverse talents and drive for continual improvement push you to seek recognition and success. Balancing the extremes of insecurity and overconfidence is key to your growth. Embrace your unique gifts and strive for equilibrium in both your personal and professional lives. Love and recognition fuel your drive, leading you to a life of purpose.

Aquarius 3: The Pragmatic Idealist

Eloquent, Expressive, Insecure, Extravagant, Generous, Romantic, Naive, Verbose, Sociable, Withdrawn, Scattered, Independent, Creative

With your knack for charm, Aquarius Threes often navigate conversations by diverting direct questions with their engaging verbosity and vibrant imagination. This skill of captivating and entertaining maintains a lively and dynamic atmosphere during interactions. You enjoy exploring various interests and prefer to keep your options open rather than choosing a single path.

You prioritise profound bonds and discovery in relationships. Despite the initial overwhelm, your goal is to find a partner who can accompany you on your journey. A balanced marriage includes both space and engaging conversation, and the decision to have children depends on your partner and the changing dynamics of your relationship.

Traditional career paths might not be a good fit for your unconventional nature. Your strengths lie in creative or non-traditional positions, and your diverse interests often prompt you to explore various industries until you uncover your ultimate purpose. Handling your finances could transform your creative skills into significant achievement.

Your unique perspective allows you to create engaging stories and innovative ideas. Harness your creativity to motivate and inspire others. When you decide based on your core values, you can create a life that is both meaningful and impactful.

Aquarius 4: The Conscientious Rebel

Innovative, Practical, Radical, Demonstrative, Informative, Constructive, Secretive, Busy, Philosophical, Determined, Insecure, Contrary, Freedom-loving, Good-hearted

Your workspace may seem disorganised to others. But, as an Aquarius Four, it shows your creative mind and unique way of organising things. Amid the chaos, you have a rare talent. You can find what you need. Clutter fuels imagination. Messy surroundings ignite fresh ideas, keeping your mind nimble and inventive.

Your irresistible charisma has a way of gathering admirers around you. Yet, your dedication to your projects and ideas can create difficulties in establishing deeper connections. Seeking more meaningful relationships requires you to take the initiative and make the first move. In a marital relationship, a collaborative partnership is important, but you do not compromise on every ground when not necessary. For you to commit to a relationship, mutual respect, engaging conversation, romance, and loyalty are crucial.

Your mind is overflowing with ideas and creativity, and a talented team brings your visions to fruition. Money holds greater significance for you than mere survival. Your inventive projects and efforts to create change rely on financial stability as a foundation.

Those around you find comfort and assurance in your unwavering nature. Embrace change and apply your wide-ranging knowledge to make positive enhancements. With your practical approach and talent for motivating others, you serve as a valuable guide in driving progress and inspiring others to take action.

Aquarius 5: The Big-Hearted Reformer

Congenial, Resourceful, Radical, Impulsive, Humane, Adventurous, Gullible, Fickle, Eloquent, Progressive, Impetuous, Restless, Scientific, Curious

Being an Aquarius Five, you combine a generous nature with a practical mindset. You are always ready to assist others, whether it's through big endeavours or small, considerate actions. Despite your preference for working behind the scenes, people value your ability to offer direction and unconventional solutions while handling tasks such as delivering aid.

In relationships, intelligence and curiosity through shared interests or chance encounters. You see life as a thrilling adventure. But, you want a modern, comfy home. You might find the idea of having children and a supportive spouse appealing, as long as you can still explore the world and maintain your freedom.

Juggling multiple interests and roles results from your desire for variety and excitement. Whether in a leadership role or as a team member, you thrive with clear objectives and the freedom to achieve them in your own style. Your diverse skills and tendency to get bored lead you to explore different fields, ranging from art to science, keeping your life dynamic and exciting.

Your ability to inspire others to reach their potential by believing in them and providing support is remarkable. Despite occasional clashes with conventional norms, your ability to provide support and believe in others, inspiring them to reach their potential, is remarkable and highly valued. However, it's crucial to maintain a balance between your individuality and relationships, so your desire for freedom doesn't seem like indifference. By embracing your role and prioritising your happiness, you can cultivate meaningful connections and a fulfilling life.

Aquarius 6: The Loyal Liberal

Informative, Responsible, Thoughtless, Outspoken, Friendly, Nurturer, Obsessive, Possessive, Generous, Seeks Harmony, Withdrawn, Self-Sacrificing, Diligent, Idealist

Aquarius Six propels itself with a mission-driven mindset, seeking to bring positive change to the world, regardless of the scale. It is evident that you are dedicated to improving life, whether you pursue innovative ideas or make simple personal changes, such as adopting a healthier diet.

Your ability to meet everyone's expectations makes you an appealing partner, but it's hard to find someone who can match this level of selflessness. You desire a relationship that blends friendship and passion, and when you meet a compatible partner, you're prepared for a lifelong commitment. The relationship you desire involves a open-minded, committed partner who can take part in diverse social groups and family activities. You provide unwavering loyalty and deep appreciation in exchange.

By having foresight, you can find a career or partner that supports your needs and allows you to express your artistic side. Your focused gaze scans the workplace, researching out any signs of unfairness or discrimination. You build your reputation as a boss by helping other's progress and respecting them as a mentor. While you can be generous, it is to support causes that help others.

Your exceptional memory allows you to recall both acts of kindness and the offences you encounter. You have a tendency to value the positive and downplay the negative, although forgiving careless or hurtful actions can be challenging for you. While encouraging others to live life to the fullest, don't forget about your own aspirations. The key to avoiding unnecessary conflict and meeting your needs is through open and honest communication.

Aquarius 7: The Cosmopolitan Charmer

Generous, Analytical, Insecure, Secretive, Philosopher, Private, Detached, Suspicious, Independent, Articulate, Radical, Aloof, Diligent, Perfectionist

Being a Aquarius Seven, you excel in both challenging the status quo and devising solutions for complex problems. With a visionary mindset, you frequently push boundaries and turn innovative ideas into reality. Like Helen Gurley Brown with *Cosmopolitan*, your unique perspective and willingness to tackle unconventional topics often lead to significant achievements.

Falling in love is a serious affair for you. You have a natural ability to sense potential in a relationship through both intuition and observation. This makes dating you a bit of a puzzle, but don't let your skepticism prevent you from exploring new possibilities. You value intellect and will be drawn to someone who stimulates your mind, though you may initially keep a bit of distance. True connection requires understanding and patience.

You are strategic and selective about your finances. You prefer to limit spending to essentials and keep your investments and savings somewhat private, even from long-term partners. Your financial approach supports your need for funding innovative projects and indulging in occasional adventures. At work, you combine practicality with thorough analysis, ensuring you approach tasks with diligence and precision.

Your enigmatic nature can make relationships with you somewhat perplexing. You value your privacy and prefer not to explain your choices or plans, which can confuse others. You understand that not everyone will grasp your vision immediately, and you often save your best ideas for later presentation. Embrace your role as a unique thinker and be mindful of how your mystery impacts those around you.

Aquarius 8: The Versatile Specialist

Cooperative, Determined, Professional, Self-defeating, Workaholic, Unbiased, Ambitious, Detached, Aggressive, Eloquent, Enduring

As an Aquarius Eight, you thrive by being versatile. Use different strategies to achieve your goals. In your quest for success, you adapt. You take on different roles and switch sides as needed. Your problem-solving style is strategic and deliberate, focusing on achieving victory.

Your approach to relationships mirrors your dedication to your career in matters of love and commitment. It is challenging to find a partner who has the same ambition and drive as you. You want to find someone who values your drive for success. They should also want a deep, meaningful connection with you. Family is important. But your career comes first. So, find a partner who supports your ambitions. Achieving work-life balance is possible with the right partner.

Your dedication, strategy, and ability to motivate others have earned you respect. Your leadership abilities are exceptional, inspiring your team and propelling them towards success. It can be a struggle to handle your finances. You excel at handling finances. But managing your finances may need more attention. You can achieve the stability you want. You could do well when you get good financial advice and commit to personal finance.

Your powerful will, strategic mind, and adaptability will lead to great success in your career and personal life. To lead a fulfilling life, it's important to balance ambition, personal life, and finances..

Your knack for advancing and playing the political game helps you achieve both joy and prosperity. You find genuine satisfaction in helping others, especially on a personal level, and enjoy mentoring those who seek your guidance. While you value independence, having a support system is crucial for maintaining your well-being and happiness. Understanding that everyone needs assistance at times, including yourself, can help you navigate both successes and setbacks with grace.

Aquarius 9: The Magnetic Mover and Shaker

Inventive, Sociable, Compassionate, Outspoken, Careless, Focused, Performer, Self-absorbed, Expressive, Charismatic

If you're an Aquarius Nine, you have a natural inclination to explore new ideas and push limits. Your belief in your skills ignites your desire for adventure. It enables you to venture out and seize new chances. There might be occasional setbacks. Your ability to be open-minded and adaptable allows you to recover from setbacks. Every experience teaches you something.

Your vivacious personality and enchanting charisma make you a captivating partner in relationships. Others may struggle to guess because of your unpredictable and unconventional approach to love. Instead, a traditional commitment is something you refuse to accept. A connection that matches your adventurous and creative personality is what you're looking for. If you desire a partnership that stimulates your intellect and passion for exploration,. Don't let conventional norms hold you back.

Your talent lies in finding profitable opportunities through various entrepreneurial endeavours. It might pose a slight challenge to manage your finances. Supporting others with your generosity can put a strain on your resources. It's important to find a balance between giving and maintaining financial stability. Your career thrives when you take charge and generate opportunities for everyone. Planning and strategy are crucial and require caution. Success is guaranteed by avoiding problems.

Your response to setbacks is both graceful and resilient. Despite unexpected outcomes, you remain dedicated to your goals. Yet, being rejected can have a deep impact on your self-esteem and emotional state. You will experience personal growth by embracing all aspects of love and relationships. It will foster a deeper understanding of yourself and those around you. Both your adventures and close connections will bring you fulfilment.

Pisces 1: The Knowledgeable Leader

Compassionate, Direct, Careless, Short-sighted, Knowledgeable, Courageous, Extremist, Inflexible, Innovative, Inventive, Procrastinates, Overbearing, Focused, Leader

As a Pisces One, you blend leadership with knowledge. Compassion and a direct approach are often how you lead. Each day, you begin with enthusiasm. To achieve balance in your life, you need to prioritise love, friendship, and business. While routine may bore you, you endure it as a necessary step toward achieving your broader goals. You enjoy challenging the status quo. You use your charm and vision to lead others through change.

In matters of the heart, falling in love is a profound experience for you. You want a romance that is both deep and meaningful. You crave a partnership that respects clear boundaries. Be the ideal partner. Welcome to a new, loving chapter in your life.

You face money confusion, grappling with its management and significance. Yet, as time goes on, you come to value it. Both the money and the recognition are important, as you can see. Your best fit for specialisation would be in a talent or profession.

Exploring new paths is something you enjoy. Moreover, your passion for utilising your creativity is to entertain others and enhance your skills.

Your personality balances seriousness with a lively, gracious demeanour. You enjoy being with others. You like to connect with friends and meet new people. But, behind closed doors, you are a dreamer. You plan, always envisioning the future. Your creativity brings fresh ideas. But you might struggle with procrastination. Others may see you as overbearing in your leadership.

Your focus and courage make you a knowledgeable leader. You can guide others with both authority and compassion, despite the challenges. Use your strengths. But be aware of your shortsightedness and rigidity. Stay adaptable and considerate as you lead and inspire others.

Pisces 2: The Mystic Matchmaker

Inspirational, Diplomatic, Procrastinator, Argumentative, Focused, Conscientious, Extremist, Sensitive, Supportive, Cynical, Worrier, Compassionate, Patient

As a Pisces Two, you excel at guarding your privacy. You use charm and wit to deflect personal questions. You're skilled at disappearing from social situations, only reappearing when it suits you. Your closest friends know your tendency to vanish for periods. They comprehend your need to stay away for work or personal time.

In love, you navigate a complex landscape. You value your freedom. Yet, you long for a deep connection with a partner. The challenge is to balance your fantasies with relationship realities. It's vital to find someone who meets both your public and private needs for happiness.

Money holds a kind of mystical allure for you. Maintaining a consistent work pace is a struggle for you. Your preference is to work only when necessary. You value roles that offer creative freedom and flexibility. Your inclination is to evade a inflexible, customary employment. You deserve a career that unleashes your inner artist and grants you freedom.

Your personal power is very strong. Yet, you often yield to others, especially in social or work situations. Notice and value yourself. Use your charisma and diplomacy. Embrace your humour and knack for reading people. But, be more consistent and open about your plans. It will help others understand you better. It will strengthen your personal and professional connections.

Pisces 3: The Sociable Statesman

Intuitive, Sociable, Frivolous, Easily Distracted, Unbiased, Creative, Lethargic, Gossipy, Inspirational, Expressive, Extravagant, Altruistic, Romantic

As a Pisces Three, you have a natural charm. It helps you cut through distractions and deliver significant results, even under pressure. This unique combination of creativity and focus makes you stand out in both your personal and professional life. Clients and bosses value your blend of charm and hard work. You always exceed their expectations.

In relationships, you value romance and tenderness. You seek deep connections, not fleeting encounters. Marriage, for you, is more than just a commitment; it's a way to build lasting friendships and add excitement to your life. It provides you with a stable foundation from which you can continue to explore new experiences and grow together with your partner.

In the business world, you're seen as a creative original. You might dream of a more relaxed life. Yet, you know the value of living well. So, you avoid getting caught up in boring tasks. Your quick learning ability and focus enable you to achieve success when you set your mind to it.

Your charisma and compassion are inspiring to those around you. You have a talent for helping others blend vision with practicality, solving problems while also planning for the future. However, be mindful of your tendency to be extravagant, in spending or praise. By balancing your generosity, you can avoid pitfalls. This will ensure your actions have a positive impact.

Pisces 4: The Capable Wizard

Empathetic, Persistent, Gullible, Methodical, Thorough, Indecisive, Serious, Knowledgeable, Practical, Temperamental, Lazy, Creative, Constructive.

As a Pisces Four, you have the unique ability to merge your imaginative dreams with practical, achievable goals. Your childhood fantasies have matured into plans. You're committed to realising them through hard work. You know how to balance your ambition with the downtime, ensuring that you maintain both your drive and your well-being.

In love, you value honesty and directness. You value genuine connections over games and shallow interactions. Marriage aligns well with your values, offering you a stable partnership where you can create a home and build a future together.

In your career, you focus on job security over the lure of high salaries. A flexible routine and a supportive work environment are essential for your happiness. You excel in roles that allow you to be hands-on and provide guidance to others. You don't seek wealth above all. But, you want a comfy life and financial stability for your family.

Your self-perception may change. You are seeking stability while enjoying traditions and celebrations that bring you joy. You value sharing responsibilities with friends, despite your independence. Collaboration can lighten your load and give you security. It can boost the support that enriches your relationships and goals.

Pisces 5: The Resourceful Dreamer

Perceptive, Resourceful, Indecisive, Impulsive, Inspirational, Progressive, Trusting, Restless, Idealistic, Curious, Escapist, Fickle, Versatile, Adventurous

As a Pisces Five, your life is a mix of imagination and reality. Dreams often turn into real outcomes. You can see possibilities where others cannot. This helps you turn your visions into reality. Your creativity can lead to impulsive choices or indecision. Trusting others may make you vulnerable to disappointment. Despite setbacks, your optimism and energy keep you going. You're always ready for the next adventure or creative task.

In matters of the heart, you seek relationships that offer both freedom and depth. Friendship is the basis of your romantic connections. You value the comfort of a close, lasting bond. Yet, you also crave the excitement and passion that keep love alive and vibrant. You thrive in relationships that allow for mutual exploration and growth. They should balance independence with intimacy. For you, marriage is not companionship. It is about a passionate, strengthening connection.

Your professional life reflects your dual needs for stability and creative expression. You can excel in conventional jobs. But, you often prefer side projects. They empower you to unleash your creativity and venture into uncharted territories of ideas. You excel at networking and charming others. Money, to you, is a tool to support your lifestyle and ambitions, rather than a primary motivation.

Your imagination and creativity possess incredible strength. They let you contribute to the world. Writing, acting, or directing has the power to inspire and educate others. The power to accomplish this lies in your unique perspective. Linking both fantasy and reality provides you with new perspectives. This makes you a valuable asset in any creative field. Embrace your dreams and use them as a guide. You can then transform your life and those around you.

Learn from your experiences. Use those lessons in your work. This will help you avoid repeating mistakes and keep growing. Your skill in blending imagination with practicality will serve you well. It will help you achieve a fulfilling, successful life while staying true to your vision.

Pisces 6: The Visionary Teacher

Altruistic, Nurturing, Procrastinates, Jealous, Versatile, Idealistic, Gullible, Self-sacrificing, Creative, Responsible, Inconsistent, Gracious, Loyal, Overbearing

As a Pisces Six, you have a rare mix of compassion and wisdom. It makes you a natural mentor and guide to those around you. Your ability to see and nurture others' potential is a defining trait. Whether you are a formal teacher or a supportive friend, you have a talent for helping others be their best.

Recognising your limits and ensuring that you meet your own needs is crucial.

Romance for you is an intricate dance between passion and stability. Despite not always wearing your heart on your sleeve, your romantic nature runs deep. You find great joy in focusing on your partner's needs. Often, you prioritise their happiness over your own. However, a balanced relationship is key to long-term fulfilment. You thrive in partnerships where both partners share a love for home life and mutual interests.

Your generosity and sense of duty can, be risky. Your desire to help others is admirable. But, it's important to set clear boundaries. Managing your finances with care and foresight will help you avoid unnecessary strain. You will find fulfilment in careers that suit your artistic, service-oriented nature. These include jobs in entertainment, medicine, art, cosmetics, and public relations. Your love for music and harmony drives you to find engaging work environments.

Your ability to inspire and uplift others is a significant strength. You have a natural talent for motivating those around you, and your enthusiasm is contagious. By embracing and refining these skills, you can continue to be a positive force in the lives of others. However, be mindful of tendencies toward possessiveness or self-criticism. Stay open to new opportunities. Also, care for yourself as you do for others.

To succeed, balance your dreams with practical efforts. You can achieve great things for yourself and those you mentor. Your kind leadership, along with good self-care and money management, will lead to a rewarding life.

Pisces 7: The Discerning Dream Weaver

Perfectionist, Analytical, Inconsistent, Aloof, Charming, Articulate, Shy, Suspicious, Knowledgeable, Intellectual, Escapist, Stingy, Methodical, Private

As a Pisces Seven, you are a blend of deep thoughtfulness and rich imagination. When alone or with a few close friends, you often introspect. You explore the depths of your mind. You love exploring topics that spark your curiosity. Your intellect drives you to understand the world.

A passionate nature lies beneath your calm and composed exterior. In romance, you seek partners who challenge you, both mind and spirit. Commitment flourishes when you immerse yourself in the union. Your partner must know that your reserved nature isn't a lack of interest. It shows a desire for a deeper connection.

Your spending habits vary. You might alternate between periods of spending and being more frugal. The most fulfilling careers are those that accommodate your perfectionism and allow for flexibility. You can excel in fields like research, writing, or any creative work. They let you explore and bring complex ideas to life. Your ability to think and innovate sets you apart.

Education and self-exploration remain key components of your growth. Don't shy away from showcasing the unique skills that define you, and have no fear of generously sharing your knowledge with others. You may doubt yourself. Don't let it hold you back. Use it to refine and improve yourself. Your grasp of complex ideas, plus your hard work, can achieve great things. These wins can inspire those around you.

Adherence to your path and faith in your abilities steer you to success. Your thoughtfulness and imagination help you navigate life's challenges with grace. As you grow, you will understand the world better. This will help you make a lasting impact on your personal life and work.

Pisces 8: The Shrewd Sifter

Professional, Sensitive, Indecisive, Romantic, Open-minded, Critical, Workaholic, Mystical, Capable, Diffident, Overreacts, Focused, Global View

As a Pisces Eight, you balance a busy schedule with ease. You stay organised and detail-oriented. Your sensitivity helps you create the right mood and handle info. But you avoid tasks unless they are necessary. Your open-mindedness helps you in complex situations. But your tendency to overreact can disrupt your focus.

In romance, you like the "diamond-in-the-rough" type. You may let first impressions sway you. You're practical and capable. But your romantic side can cause you to idealise new relationships. It's striking when someone makes a surprising impression on you. Your shyness can make you indecisive. But your desire for deep connections drives you to seek balance in love.

You begin by acquiring financial insight, refining skills along the way. Your workaholic ways make you watch your finances. You work hard to stay grounded. Your critical eye helps you understand financial details. This keeps you stable.

Your growth has sped up. You've balanced family, personal needs, and business with a global view. Your responsibilities can be overwhelming. But your insight and positivity inspire others. Your ability to turn dreams into reality is a key strength. So is your skill at managing complex tasks.

Your mix of practicality and creativity makes you a natural leader. You are also professional and focused. Use your unique strengths. Keep using your skills to find success and fulfilment.

Pisces 9: The Perceptive Performer

Visionary, Charismatic, Versatile, Demanding, Artistic, Perceptive, Creative, Worldly

As a Pisces Nine, you dream big. You aim for great things and push beyond limits. Your vision and talents drive you to achieve great things. But high expectations and a wandering mind can cause some inactivity and dissatisfaction. Embracing your visionary ideas while managing practical challenges is key.

In romance, you may feign disinterest in marriage. You desire a partner with refined style and a relaxed demeanour. You find charismatic, smart people fascinating. But past disappointments make you wary of commitment. Fantasy and romance are key. Yet, balancing them with reality helps form lasting connections.

Your investments yield unpredictable returns, causing financial fluctuations. You excel at spotting future trends. But, consult financial experts before major decisions to manage your finances better. Your generosity and loyalty to friends are notable. Maintain a solid financial foundation to avoid debt.

You love the mysteries of life and the cosmos. But, you need to connect with others. To achieve your goals, balance visionary ideas with practical actions. Embrace change. Be kind to yourself. Be flexible. Use these to guide yourself and others to success as things change.

Astrology and numerology offer valuable insights into a person's character and approach to life. Even without personal information, they provide valuable insights. This method presents a broad, yet effective approach to gaining insight into someone's essential attributes and behaviours.

Take, for instance, an ambitious and imaginative individual who seeks to explore uncharted territory and attain remarkable accomplishments. Combining their romantic tendencies and carefulness implies a blend of imagination and realism in matters of the heart. They want a partner who understands their vision and respects their past.

Their riches change with every change in investment strategy. Their proactive and perceptive approach underscores the main point. Balancing generosity and financial prudence is crucial.

Seeking expert advice can help them better manage their complex finances.

Astrology and numerology offer a detailed perspective on an individual's strengths, obstacles, and aspirations. This perspective reveals their traits and abilities. It provides a firm foundation for more meaningful connections and interactions.

Chapter 6 : Basic Character Traits

As you prepare for marriage, look beyond the corporate facade. It's crucial to exercise caution when meeting someone new in person. Develop a deliberate plan for meetings, clarifying arrangements with your partner. This prep helps create a safe space for genuine connections. It also reduces risks. You will understand your partner better. A good way to learn their true character is to spend time together outside of work. A simple yet revealing gesture is to invite your partner to dinner in a casual setting, away from the office. This small action can reveal parts of their personality. The employees could hide in the corporate environment.

Why is this important? Experts often suggest that watching your partner in social settings, outside work, can reveal their true nature. We explore why this exercise is key to a better understanding of your partner. It helps build a respectful, loving, and harmonious relationship.

- **Observing Respect for Others**: When you take your partner to a restaurant, watch how they treat the staff: the server, the chef, and the gate personnel. Do they exhibit kindness, patience, and respect towards these individuals? How they treat people in service roles can be a powerful indicator of their true character. Respectful behaviour shows empathy, humility, and a concern for others' feelings. These are vital qualities in a lifelong partner.

- **Adapting to Unfamiliar Environments**: Assess your partner's behaviour outside work. It helps you gauge their adaptability and flexibility. In a corporate setting, people can hide their true selves. But, in an unfamiliar place, their true nature may emerge. Their ability to adjust to different situations shows their versatility. It shows a willingness to compromise for a harmonious relationship.

- **Authenticity and Transparency**: Outside of work, your partner may drop their facade. This allows you to witness their true, authentic version. Do they express their opinions and feelings, or do they continue to wear a mask? Authenticity and transparency are crucial in building trust and intimacy within a marriage. Watching your partner in relaxed social settings reveals their true selves.

- **Relationship Building**: These after-work dinners help you bond by sharing stories and experiences. They can help build a sense of community outside of work. As you near marriage, it may help. It is an investment in your partnership. It could deepen and please your bond.

- **Evaluating Problem-Solving Skills:** Another key aspect to observe is how your partner handles unexpected challenges in a casual setting. Life is full of surprises, and how someone deals with minor inconveniences, like a delayed order at a restaurant or a sudden change in plans, can offer insights into their problem-solving abilities. Do they remain calm and composed, or do they react with frustration? A partner who can navigate these small hurdles with grace is likely to be more resilient when facing bigger challenges in your relationship.

- **Emotional Intelligence:** Finally, pay attention to your partner's emotional intelligence during these outings. Emotional intelligence encompasses the ability to recognise, understand, and manage one's own emotions, as well as the emotions of others. Observe how your partner responds to the emotions of those around them, including yours. Do they show empathy when someone is upset? Are they capable of offering comfort or support when needed? High emotional intelligence is essential for a nurturing and fulfilling marriage, as it fosters better communication, understanding, and emotional connection between partners.

Leaving the corporate world and seeing your partner in social settings shows their true character. Observing how they interact with others can reveal their true selves. It can also show how they adapt to new environments. This understanding is key to building a strong, respectful, and loving relationship. On this journey, deepen your connection. Build a partnership based on understanding and respect.

As we end, it's important to think about the profound knowledge we've gained from exploring this book together. Getting married is a major decision that requires mutual understanding, respect, and love to thrive. In the book, we explored looking beyond the corporate facade we wear at work. The success of your relationship relies on seeing and understanding your partner, not just their public image.

We've discussed spending time together in relaxed settings, where people can reveal their true character. By sharing meals, facing unforeseen obstacles, and observing their interactions, you gain valuable insights into your partner's character, values, and emotional intelligence. This discovery process serves a purpose beyond just identifying faults or flaws.

Remember, the focus is on understanding, not passing judgement. Trust, empathy, and growth together form strong relationships. Remember, these lessons as you continue your journey. Approach with an open mind, communicate, and cherish the love that united you. When you do this, you're not just getting ready for a wedding day, but you're also setting the foundation for a lifelong partnership characterised by respect, harmony, and mutual growth.

A True Relationship means both partners feeling acknowledged, listened to, and respected for their true selves. It's a relationship where both of you can grow together, facing life's challenges hand in hand. As you begin your journey into marriage, may you always appreciate and value the special qualities that make your partner the one you want to be with forever. May this understanding form establishing an enduring love.

About the Author

Santtu Roy holds the position of Senior Solution Full-Stack Architect. With a specialisation in OpenAI and GenAI, he has accumulated 18 years of IT experience. Santtu has expertise in designing and developing full-stack, microservice-based systems. He specialises in

infrastructure as Code (IAC), ITSM, and the automation of networks and data centers. In addition, he is knowledgeable in DevOps and blockchain dApps. Python is where his expertise lies. He is skilled in machine learning, deep learning, NLP, LLMs, and data science. Skilled in various technologies, such as MERN, he released his debut book, "The Power of Self Brainwash," in 2018, receiving praise from both readers and critics. "Unlocking Your Destiny," his numerology book published in 2022, delves into tapping into one's true potential and fulfilling their destiny, reflecting his fascination with self-care, Numerology, Astrology and spirituality.